Mental Aerobics

MENTAL AEROBICS

Exercises for a Stronger, Healthier Mind

B. Alexis Castorri, M.S.

AND

Jane Heller

PHOTOGRAPHS BY MICHAEL FORESTER

A Citadel Press Book
Published by Carol Publishing Group

A Citadel Press Book
Published by Carol Publishing Group
Citadel Press is a registered trademark of Carol Communications, Inc.
Editorial Offices: 600 Madison Avenue, New York, N.Y. 10022
Sales and Distribution Offices: 120 Enterprise Avenue, Secaucus, N.J.
  07094
In Canada: Canadian Manda Group, P.O. Box 920, Station U, Toronto,
  Ontario M8Z 5P9
Queries regarding rights and permissions should be addressed to Carol
Publishing Group, 600 Madison Avenue, New York, N.Y. 10022

Carol Publishing Group books are available at special discounts for bulk
purchases, for sales promotions, fund raising, or educational purposes.
Special editions can be created to specifications. For details, contact
Special Sales Department, Carol Publishing Group, 120 Enterprise
Avenue, Secaucus, N.J. 07094

Manufactured in the United States of America

10 9 8 7 6 5 4 3 2 1

Library of Congress Cataloging-in-Publication Data

Castorri, B. Alexis.
     Mental aerobics : excercises for a stronger, healthier mind /
B. Alexis Castorri and Jane Heller.
               p.   cm.
     "A Citadel Press Book."
     ISBN 0-8065-1362-4 (pbk.)
     1. Mental discipline. I. Heller, Jane II. Title.
BF632.C37   1992   92-31422
153.4'2—dc20   CIP

To my parents, Albert and Dora
B.A.C.

To Godie Forester
J.H.

CONTENTS

1 / Warming Up   4

2 / Exercises for the Workplace   15

3 / Exercises for Romantic Relationships 37

4 / Exercises for Adult-Child Relationships 56

5 / Exercises for General Mental Fitness 74

6 / Cooling Down 92

ACKNOWLEDGMENTS

There are several people who've assisted and supported me in the preparation of this book, and I'd like to extend a heartfelt thanks to each of them: literary agent Jane Dystel, whose professionalism I greatly admire; Carol Publishing's Bruce Shostak, who offered insights and advice throughout the process; my colleagues at Lauderdale Psychological Services—David Burkhead, Ph.D., Vincel Herlovich, M.S., John Reininger, M.S., Diana Brady, M.S., Gail Fantaci, M.S., and Judy Regner, office manager—who make me proud to work in the field of psychology; Alan S. Becker and Filip Krajcik, who challenged me to begin this book; Mike Joyce, who lent support early on; Mauricio Gonzalez Sommella, whose presence in my life inspired me to finish the book; my "mental coaches"—Judy Fisher, Peggy Van Vlack, Carol Mirabel, Rosalie Titone, Dottie Wegelin, Aurora, and Janus— who gave me spiritual guidance; and all my clients, from whom I continue to learn.

Complete credit for the original concept of "an exercise manual for the mind" goes to my coauthor and friend, Jane Heller. When she approached me about writing *Mental Aerobics* in November 1990, I didn't know which would be more intimidating for me: going public with my work or working with this formidable veteran of the New York publishing scene. It turned out that Jane was a dynamic, gifted writer and "idea broker" who provided constant encouragement, enlightened criticism, and spirited friendship at every point along the way. Prior to collaborating with Jane on *Mental Aerobics*, I'd always flown solo on projects, preferring to research, experiment, and produce on my own. But pooling our collective resources and talents—not to mention personalities—was an absolute delight for me. To have had my ideas not only articulated but improved upon was an experience for which I'll always be grateful.

Alexis Castorri

This book could not have been written without the help of the following people: Cindy Shmerler, who put me in touch with my coauthor-to-be; Bruce Shostak, who believed in the project, and Jane Dystel, who hung in there until the deal was done. Special thanks, of course, to the ingenious Alexis Castorri, whose talent as a therapist is eclipsed only by her devotion as a friend.

Jane Heller

FOREWORD

When I first met Alexis Castorri in January of 1984, I was at an interesting point in my career.

Having beaten John McEnroe the summer before at the French Open final in Paris, my ranking at the age of twenty-four was number three in the world. I wanted to be number one. So, following that match, I made a commitment to myself to improve as many aspects of my game as possible. One of the things I did was to change my diet to improve my physical conditioning. Another thing I did was to begin working with Alexis to improve my mental conditioning.

Although I was Alexis's first professional athlete-client, she had been working in the area of mental conditioning for several years in her private practice. Over a seven-month period, she designed a series of mental exercises for my use, all of which were extremely effective and none of which took more than 15 to 20 minutes a few times a day—a time commitment anyone who is serious about working on his or her mental outlook can make.

Among the specific exercises Alexis taught me was one called "Increasing Your Powers of Focus and Concentration," which is included in this book. I had asked her to show me how to heighten my ability to focus during a match, and this exercise was very effective in accomplishing that goal. It helped me develop a total focus whenever I really needed to zero in on the ball and block out all outside distractions. Top tennis players always focus on the ball to some extent, but every player knows that there are distinctly different levels of focus that come and go during a match. After several weeks of doing Alexis's exercise, which involved staring at and observing every detail of various small objects around the house, I found that I could deepen my level of focus on the court when I really needed to.

Another mental exercise I found to be very effective was the one Alexis calls "Overcoming Minor Daily Frustrations." It, too, is in this book. It involves detailing the components of an event or activity, then stepping outside yourself and describing your participation in the event in the third person. For example, if I'm playing a tough match and want to focus my concentration, I might say to myself, "Ivan is walking over to the chair and getting a towel to dry off. Now Ivan is walking back toward the service line. Now he is putting his hand in his pocket to get some sawdust. Now he is wiping the grip of his racquet with the sawdust," and so on, until the objective of my next action is clear. Players have to deal with lots of emotions during close matches, but this exercise allowed me to channel them for maximum effect on my performance.

I also derived great benefit from some of the warming-up exercises featured in *Mental Aerobics*. One that I used at the beginning of my work with Alexis was called "Limbering Up With Timed Counting." Counting seconds as you stare at the face of a watch sounded simple to me, but I remember feeling as if I were working "mental muscles" I'd never worked before. I'd do Alexis's mental warm-ups each morning, and by the time I'd get to the court for practice, my mind was stretched and ready to make the most of each minute of play.

Most of you who are reading *Mental Aerobics* won't be making the finals of a Grand Slam tennis tournament, but all of you have arenas of performance in which you'd like to excel—whether it's the corporate boardroom, the college classroom, or the family kitchen. No matter what your profession or lifestyle, you're going to be mentally tested out in the world. *Mental Aerobics* is doable, interesting, and fun—a pathway to success whose only limitations are those you create in your mind.

Greenwich, Connecticut   **Ivan Lendl**

PREFACE

I don't know if everyone who attended high school in the sixties confronted his identity crisis armed with Hermann Hesse's *Siddhartha*, but I did. What's more, after immersing myself in many of Hesse's dreamy, mystical stories, I came to the conclusion that the world of the mind was definitely a place I wanted to explore. So I read and reread books about philosophy, psychology, Eastern religions—you name it.

One book that made an indelible impression on me was Carl Rogers's *On Becoming a Person*. Rogers, a psychotherapist, introduced the concept of "client-centered therapy," in which the client heals himself while the therapist simply facilitates the process. This theory appealed to my sixteen-year-old sensibilities, probably because it suggested that I could find my solution to my identity not out in the world or among my peers, but somewhere within my own mind.

By the time I wrote my senior term paper comparing Jean Paul Sartre's existential beliefs to those of Jewish theologian Martin Buber, I was as intellectual as a painfully naive teenager could be.

As a college student I continued to be fascinated by the power of the mind. I remember enrolling in a metaphysical literature class and reading a short story by a French writer named Robbe-Grillet. Its theme was a conventional life-and-death conflict, but its plot offered an interesting twist: At the end of the story the reader discovered that the protagonist was actually a figment of another character's imagination, a symbol of someone else's dream.

Dreams, symbols, ideas, and other products of the human

mind held my interest throughout my youth. Then came my turbulent twenties, when I put my intellect on hold and decided to *live*! For nearly a decade I worked at various jobs and traveled around the world, only to turn thirty, return to Fort Lauderdale, Florida, where I grew up, and became a mental health counselor.

I don't know why it took so long to rediscover my adolescent interest in the study of the mind, but once it reemerged, I embraced it unreservedly by opening a private practice and specializing in child and family therapy. I found myself combining Carl Rogers's theory (we *do* hold our own answers deep within our minds) with a healthy dose of Eastern philosophy (we *can* learn to increase our mental focus and concentration) to help my clients solve an array of psychological problems. My hybrid approach seemed to work.

Then, in the winter of 1984, a friend introduced me to tennis star Ivan Lendl, who was in Florida for the Lipton International Tournament. I went to watch Ivan play and, after the match, had dinner with him. During the meal, we talked at length about the many ways people could strengthen their minds in order to overcome a wide variety of problems.

Three nights later, Ivan called me. He was scheduled to play Stefan Edberg the next day and was concerned that Edberg's kick serve and the predicted windy conditions might cost him the match. "Remember our discussion about mind control the other evening?" he asked. "Is there any way that I could visualize Edberg's serve so it won't seem intimidating to me?" I said yes and created a mental exercise for Ivan on the spot. But I cautioned him that he might not see dramatic results from one brief telephone conversation.

Ivan lost that match but phoned to say that he did notice a major improvement in his ability to view his opponent's serve in a less threatening way. "Do you have any more of those mental exercises?" he asked.

I said I did and agreed to create an entire program of

mental and physical aerobics for him over an eight-month period.

We began to work together, sometimes through long-distance phone conversations, often at his home in Greenwich, Connecticut. Soon, he started winning more tournaments and beating players he hadn't beaten before. At the end of the summer, he defeated his longtime rival John McEnroe at the U.S. Open. The victory cinched his ranking as the number one player in the world and established him as the fittest player in the game—mentally and physically.

My work with Ivan led to extensive media coverage of my unique "mental aerobics" concept. Over the next few years, I continued to define and refine the mental exercises I was prescribing for my clients, who now included professional men and women who had read about the Lendl program and wanted the same leg up on their opponents, not on a tennis court, but in the business arena. These clients expressed a keen interest in learning to do what Ivan did—overcome mental obstacles by strengthening the mind. I thought, why not create exercises that would encourage anyone—athletes, businessmen and women, housewives, parents, children—to function at their highest mental levels?

At my clients' insistence, I created mental exercises for dozens of everyday problems—exercises addressing everything from becoming a more creative thinker to conquering fear. I never let on that many of these exercises were drawn from Eastern philosophy; I didn't want my clients to think I was asking them to give up their Cuisinarts and BMWs to join the ranks of Tibetan monks! But the truth is, the exercises were built on the Eastern idea of "going within yourself." I've just adapted them for our Western I-want-what-I-want-when-I-want-it mentality.

Why should we go within ourselves? What's my goal here? I want to help my clients—and now you, the reader of this book—improve their minds the same way athletes develop their bodies. By stretching, toning, warming up, and cooling down, you can build new strength and agility to apply to life's everyday problems. That's what this mental workout book is all about. It's a how-to manual that trains the mind to perform at its best in real-life situations.

And speaking of real-life situations, the years ahead are going to provide us with challenges and demands we never thought we'd have to face. Competition for high-paying jobs will get tighter. Pressures on the nuclear family will get more intense. Uncertainties about health and personal safety will grow. And the more technologically sophisticated we become, the greater the number of problems our minds will have to solve.

Mental Aerobics won't solve these problems, but it will help you deal with them. It's simply one more weapon in your arsenal of self-help skills, a weapon that will train your mind to operate at a higher, more efficient level than it has in the past.

Mental Aerobics is not a substitute for psychotherapy, which I continue to practice with those clients who require a more traditional approach to self-discovery. It is intended for functioning individuals who are looking for accessible, effective, easy-to-do methods of achieving better emotional and mental health.

Why not look over the exercises that follow to see if any of them addresses a challenge you're facing or a problem you'd like to tackle? I have a hunch that many of them will strike a chord—and that, by doing the exercises, you'll experience the same quick results my clients have over the years.

B.A.C.

Mental Aerobics

INTRODUCTION

How, When, and Where Do You Do Mental Aerobics?

It is said that while the human mind is the most magnificent machine ever created, we have yet to tap its full potential.

This book of exercises is designed to help you tap the full potential of *your* mind. Even if you already consider yourself "mentally fit," you'll find that after taking a few minutes each day to perform these exercises, you'll notice a remarkable improvement in your ability to face the problems and challenges of your daily life.

The beauty of mental aerobics is that, unlike physical workouts, they don't require special clothing or an expensive membership at a health club, and they can be done in complete privacy—without strangers checking out your every move. You won't be in competition with anyone when you do mental aerobics; your goal will be simply to stretch and tone your mental muscles.

Like physical workouts, the mental exercises in this book fall under several categories. Just as physical workouts allow you to stretch and tone specific areas of the body (hips, stomach, thighs, etc.), mental aerobics allow you to work on specific areas of your life (work, romance, parenting, etc.). And just as physical workouts begin with warm-up routines and end with cool-down techniques, this book features a complete menu of warm-ups and cool-downs for the mind.

1

When you turn to the individual chapters of exercises, you'll notice that each exercise is preceded by a description of the *benefits* you will derive from performing that exercise, the *time* you should reasonably allot for the exercise, the *equipment* or props you may need, and the *body position* or physical posture you should assume for maximum benefit and comfort.

To help you get started, here are answers to some questions you may have about performing mental aerobics:

How Do I Do Mental Aerobics?

- With your conscious mind. There are no exercises in the book that are meant to dip into your subconscious through any form of hypnosis, although several of the exercises will leave you feeling as calm and relaxed as if you had been hypnotized.
- With an alert, sober mind. Don't expect to derive full benefit from these exercises if you perform them after throwing back a few beers or getting wound up from drinking several cups of coffee.
- With an attitude of openness and adventure. There are no hidden or subliminal agendas in this book—just plain mental workouts that offer you another weapon in your arsenal of problem-solving techniques.
- With patience. You may feel some resistance to performing these exercises; after all, your mind is used to working out its problems in the same old way and you'll be throwing it a curve by asking it to stretch in new directions.

When Do I Do Mental Aerobics?

- Whenever you feel overwhelmed by current or long-range pressures.
- Whenever you feel your focus and concentration slipping.
- Whenever you'd like to attack an emotional problem with logic.

- Whenever you want to break old patterns and think more creatively.
- Whenever you need to relax.
- Whenever you want to recharge your mental energy. These exercises can be performed anytime, day or night. Before each exercise, I'll give you my suggestions for appropriate times of the day, but they're only *my* suggestions. Feel free to experiment and find the times that make the most sense for you.

Where Do I Do Mental Aerobics?
- Anywhere that's relatively quiet, where you're not likely to be disturbed. Some exercises require more quiet than others, but you should choose the environments that work best for you. There's no need for you to install a special "mind gym" or "mental workout room" in your home or office. In fact, many of the exercises can be done in a doctor's waiting room, at a supermarket checkout counter, you name it! No matter where you choose to perform each exercise, I suggest that you complete *all* the steps of the exercise. Don't break your concentration by taking a phone call, answering the door, or putting dinner in the oven. Finish the entire exercise before going on with your daily routine; interrupting your mind during its aerobic workout will only lessen the overall benefits of the workout.

Good luck—or, as a famous exercise guru once said, "Go for the burn!"

1

Warming Up

If you've ever joined an aerobics class, been a member of a gym, or participated in competitive sports, you know that the first activity your teacher, trainer, or coach instructs you to do is a series of stretching exercises designed to limber up your muscles—exercises that are usually followed by cardio-vascular activities designed to get your heart pumping at a slightly faster than normal rate.

The purpose of "warm-up" activities is to slowly acclimate your sedentary body to the more strenuous workout that lies ahead. In this chapter you'll find exercises that represent the mental equivalent of physical warm-up routines. In this case, warming up your mind means "getting the fuzzies out" before you begin your day or before you tackle a mentally demanding project—from preparing for a business meeting to planning a dinner party.

Serious athletes have learned that they can get more out of their workouts if they take the time to prepare their bodies first; warming up allows them to train longer and harder and, therefore, perform more effectively when it really counts.

Warming up your mind will allow *you* to perform more effectively when it really counts. How often do you not fully wake up until you've been at the office for a few hours? How often do you not fully wake up until the day is almost over? Imagine the benefits you'd derive if you could *gain* an hour or two of sharp, focused thought each and every day.

4

The exercises in this chapter will help you warm up specific mental functions that are crucial to your daily routine: list making, numerical thinking, word visualization and comprehension, and memory.

Start out by reading the "benefit" section of each exercise and then decide which warm-up is right for you on a particular day. You can do one exercise each day or perform all five—it's up to you. I encourage you to try them all at least once, as they are proven devices for jump-starting your mind. Then, after you've become familiar with these warmups, you might want to combine them with other exercises in the book (i.e., pair the warm-up exercise called "Getting Your Mind in Gear" with the workplace exercise called "Achieving Championship-Level Thinking"). And if you want to increase your mental warm-up, by all means do so, either by performing an exercise more than once a day or by adding a minute or two to the length of the exercise.

I think you'll discover, as my clients do, that your mind is loose, alert, and ready for action after you do these warmups.

WARM-UP EXERCISE 1

Getting Your Mind in Gear

Benefit: Whenever you start a physical workout program with 5–10 minutes of stretching exercises, the idea is to get in gear before moving on to more strenuous activities. The same theory applies here. Think of this exercise as your morning "mental warm-up"—an exercise that wakes up your mind for the many mental tasks that await you in your busy day.

Time: 5–10 minutes first thing upon awakening.

Equipment Needed: None.

Body Position: Sitting comfortably or lying down.

* * *

Step 1: Count out loud backward from 100 to 1, *as quickly as you can*. If you make a mistake, continue on. Don't stop.

Step 2: Recite the alphabet out loud, giving each letter a word partner ("A–apple, B–basket, C–continue, D–don't, E–everyone," etc.). Do this step *as quickly as you can*. If you hesitate for 30 seconds or more on a particular letter of the alphabet, skip it and keep moving. Speed is important here. (If you plan on doing this exercise every morning and find yourself prone to repeating certain words, don't worry: This is not a vocabulary test!)

Step 3: Name out loud twenty men's names *as quickly as you can*, numbering them as you go ("1–Philip, 2–Joe, 3–Robert, 4–Michael, 5–Peter," etc.).

Step 4: Name out loud twenty women's names *as quickly as you can*, numbering them as you did in STEP 3.

Step 5: Name out loud twenty types of food *as quickly as you can*, numbering them as you did in STEPS 3 and 4 ("1–banana, 2–hamburger, 3–Jell-O, 4–rice, 5–mayonnaise," etc.).

Step 6: Choose one letter of the alphabet and name twenty words that begin with that letter *as quickly as you can*, numbering them as you go ("1–morning, 2–mother, 3–massage, 4–miss, 5–mope," etc.).

Step 7: If your eyes were open during the exercise, that's fine, but close them now. Count to 20 and open them. Your mind is now warmed up, stretched out, and ready for the day.

Note: If you do this exercise for several weeks and find yourself tiring of the categories of lists I've suggested, by all means create your own categories. Decide at the beginning of the exercise what your lists will be, though, as the exercise loses its effectiveness if you stop, hesitate, or think. If you plan to do this exercise before getting out of bed in the morning, try writing the day's categories on a piece of paper and keeping the list by your bed so that once you begin the exercise, you can move quickly from one category to another. If you create your own lists, keep them descriptive and in no way a reminder of burdens, responsibilities, or chores (like "Twenty things I need to buy at the grocery store today").

———————

WARM-UP EXERCISE 2

Limbering Up With Timed Counting

Benefit: This mental warm-up is a moderate stretch for your mind—an exercise to be performed *after* you've awakened, had your breakfast, read the paper, and are preparing yourself for the day. In this exercise your mind will focus on the simple process of counting, although instead of counting forward from 1 to 100, you'll be using a watch's second hand and counting in sync with the seconds ticking. This exercise effectively warms up the mind because all mathematical activities—including counting—are great for rehearsing the mind for such sequential daily activities as (believe it or not) opening the car door, getting into the car, putting the key in the ignition, and starting the motor.

Time: 5 minutes, preferably in the morning.

Equipment Needed: A watch with a second hand.

Body Position: Sitting.

*   *   *

Step 1: Sit in a comfortable, straight-backed chair, if possible, and place the watch on a flat surface in front of you (a desk or table). You should be close enough to the watch to see its second hand easily. If you prefer, you can hold the watch in front of you with one or both hands.

Step 2: When the second hand reaches the twelve o'clock position (at the top of the watch), begin counting the seconds out loud, not in their normal sequence, but in *even* numbers only (i.e., "2–4–6–8–10" and so on). Make sure you're counting in sync with the seconds ticking (i.e., one number for each second). When one minute is up, go on to the next step.

Step 3: For the second minute of this exercise, count the seconds out loud in *odd* numbers only (i.e., "1–3–5–7–9" and so on). When the second hand returns to twelve o'clock, go on to the next step.

Step 4: For the third minute of this exercise, repeat STEP 2 (counting *even* numbers in sync with the seconds ticking). When the second hand reaches twelve o'clock, go on to STEP 5.

Step 5: For the fourth minute of this exercise, repeat STEP 3 (counting *odd* numbers in sync with the seconds ticking). When the second hand reaches twelve o'clock, go on to STEP 6.

Step 6: The fifth minute of this exercise is simple: Just count the seconds in their normal sequential order (numbers 1–60), making sure you're counting in sync with the seconds ticking. This step functions as a sort of "cool-down," allowing your mind to slow down and prepare for the day ahead.

Note: Don't panic if you miss several seconds as the second hand is sweeping around the face of the watch. Just pick up where you fumbled and keep going; don't hesitate or stop. The goal of this exercise is to limber up and stretch your mind by focusing your attention on two things at once: counting in particular sequences and counting to a particular rhythm.

———————————————

WARM-UP EXERCISE 3

Exercising Memory Muscles

Benefit: Every day we deposit millions of bits of data into our short- and long-term memory banks. As we get older, it becomes more and more difficult to retrieve this data when we need it, not only because "information overload" worsens as the years go by, but because our ability to memorize information worsens as we are further removed from the school experience, where we were *forced* to memorize information for spelling bees or history quizzes. The fact is, we've fallen "out of practice" when it comes to memorizing bits of information. Before we know it, we can't remember somebody's name at a social function, or where we put our car keys, or what we were supposed to buy at the grocery store. In other words, our memory muscles have grown flabby! What can be done about these sagging memory muscles? Exercise them! They need to be worked and stretched just like any other muscles—otherwise they'll atrophy. This simple exercise will allow you to work and stretch your memory muscles as you go about your daily activities. After performing the exercise regularly, you'll see a noticeable difference in your ability to dip into your memory bank and retrieve facts, figures, names, and faces when you need them.

Time: Approximately 5 minutes several times a day. The more often you do the exercise, the sharper your memory will become.

Equipment Needed: None.

Body Position: As the exercise dictates.

*   *   *

Step 1: To do this exercise, you need to create a series of memory "mini-quizzes" as you go about your day. Begin by taking 2–3 minutes to mentally record several pieces of information that are easily accessible during your normal routine. Say to yourself, "I commit this information to memory."

Step 2: Look away, walk away, or simply close your eyes. Then list the material you memorized. Take another 2–3 minutes for this step.

Sample memory mini-quizzes include:

1. While sitting in your office, open a file drawer, commit twenty file names to memory, say to yourself, "I commit this information to memory,"and close the drawer. Then close your eyes and list the file names in the order in which you memorized them. Open the drawer and check your list.

2. While shopping in a grocery store, walk down the cereal aisle, commit fifteen cereal brand names to memory in the order in which they appear on the shelf, say to yourself, "I commit this information to memory," and walk away. Then list the cereal brand names in the order in which you memorized them. Several minutes later, go back down the cereal aisle and check your list.

3. While reading the morning paper, turn to the financial page, commit ten to twenty company stock quotes to memory, say to yourself, "I commit this information to memory," and put the paper down. Get up and finish dressing or drinking your coffee. Then list as many of the stock quotes as you have memorized. Several minutes later pick up the newspaper and check your list.

Note: For the most part, these examples work and stretch your short-term memory. If you wish to exercise your long-term memory, commit the information to memory as you would in the examples above, but instead of quizzing yourself minutes later, wait several *days* or *weeks* to test your memory.

Warm-Up Exercise 4

Racewalking Your Mind

Benefit: One of the most effective ways to warm up the mind is to make it work faster. This exercise accomplishes that goal by pitting your mind against the clock in a kind of racewalking contest during which your mind must make word associations before the allotted time runs out. The concept was borrowed from my high school composition teacher, who used to give us a noun and then ask us to write about the word for 30 minutes—without stopping! A pared down version of that assignment, this exercise is a superb mental warm-up because it forces the mind to work at a high rate of speed while conjuring up verbal images. Do the exercise in the morning before your day begins, or perform it right before you sit down to work on a project that requires mental sharpness (composing a presentation, grinding out a legal brief, constructing a marketing strategy, etc.).

Time: 5 minutes.

Equipment Needed: Pen and paper; kitchen timer, alarm clock, or wristwatch.

Body Position: Sitting is most comfortable.

* * *

Step 1: Pick up any form of printed material that's lying around your home or office, and quickly, without much thought, select a noun (e.g., you pick up the morning paper and spot the word *frost* on the weather page).

Step 2: Get out your paper and pen and sit down in a comfortable place. Set the timer or alarm clock to ring after 5 minutes. (If you're at work and don't have access to either, simply glance at your wristwatch and mark a 5-minute time period.)

Step 3: At the top of the sheet of paper, write the noun you've selected. For the next 5 minutes, write as many phrases or words as you can think of that include or incorporate this noun. Do this *as quickly as possible*. Don't let your pen leave the paper. Don't stop to analyze or think about what you're writing. Just keep writing! See the examples below:

Frost

Jack Frost	frosty ice-cream cone
frostbitten	frosty emotions
frost on a windowsill	defrost the refrigerator
windshield frost	David Frost

At the end of the 5 minutes, stop, "shake out" your mind by counting from 1 to 20, get up, stretch your body, and go on with your day.

Note: Don't worry if your words or phrases seem silly or vague, and don't pay much attention to grammar or syntax. The point of this exercise is to force your mind to move at high speed, so stopping to make corrections would be counterproductive to your mental warm-up.

WARM-UP EXERCISE 5

Stretching Your Brain to the Max

Benefit: The beauty of this brain stretch is that it offers you a verbal workout (it activates your ability to recognize and comprehend words), a visual workout (it stimulates your ability to hold a picture in your mind), and a perceptual workout (it heightens your ability to make sense of that picture)—all at the same time. Stretching your verbal, visual, and perceptual skills is an excellent method for warming up

your mind for a tough day ahead. If this mental workout seems too strenuous, don't panic. Remember that before stepping up to the plate to hit, a baseball player warms up in the on-deck circle by swinging two or three bats at the same time. When he drops the additional weight and switches to one bat, he finds that his range of movement has increased and his muscles can handle the bat with ease.

Time: 10 minutes daily.

Equipment Needed: Printed reading material—a book, magazine, or newspaper.

* * *

Step 1: This exercise has only one step. For 10 minutes daily hold some form of printed reading material in front of you *upside down* and read the words from this position. Immediately you will notice that your reading speed and comprehension decrease dramatically as your brain struggles to "right" the words. Normally able to perceive words at a fast pace, your brain must now work harder in order to accomplish the task at hand. But reading quickly is not the task here; stretching the brain is.

2

Exercises for the Workplace

Many of the men and women I've counseled derive much of their identity from their careers, which I believe is true for most of us. Think about how important your job is to your identity: Your title describes your rank in your company's hierarchy; your salary or commission tells you how valuable you are to your employer, not to mention how able you are to pay your bills; your ability to play office politics demonstrates your ability to survive in the world at large; and, of course, your choice of job reflects your interests, talents, and level of education. Even the way you refer to your "nine-to-five life"—whether you say, "my career," "my profession," or "my job"—provides insight into how you view yourself.

No matter what your job—CEO, free-lancer, student—your self-esteem is undoubtedly tied to your performance at that job. That's why I've devoted this chapter to situations that arise on the job. The exercises here represent many of the challenges you're sure to face when heading out into the great, wild workplace. My goal was to design mental exercises that will maximize your innate ability to do the work you have already chosen. Several of the exercises were borrowed from my work with professional athletes, who must compete all year long under high-stakes conditions. You may not be a tennis player who can blow $100,000 on one lousy shot, but you may be a hard worker who can blow a promotion on a lousy sales presentation.

15

The exercises in this chapter will help you increase your powers of focus and concentration, develop greater mental stamina, feel comfortable asking for a raise or promotion, avoid friction with coworkers, conquer public speaking jitters, think more creatively, and learn how to *will* yourself to succeed the same way champions do. My professional clients swear by these exercises. I'm sure you'll achieve the same great results.

But before forging ahead, keep in mind that these exercises—as well as those in other chapters—have applications beyond their specific chapter. In other words, you'll find that exercises designed to help you in the workplace can be just as useful in other areas of your life. "Increasing Your Powers of Focus and Concentration," for example, can be used whenever you need to sharpen your focus—from studying for a history exam to lowering your golf score. "Asking for a Raise or Promotion" can teach you how to stand up for yourself, whether to a mate or a sibling. "Avoiding Friction with Coworkers" can help anyone deal with a difficult person—from a meddling in-law to a snobby neighbor. And "Achieving Championship-Level Thinking" isn't just for setting and attaining professional milestones; it will encourage you to stick to a diet, train for an athletic contest, or reach for a goal you've dreamed of accomplishing.

WORKPLACE EXERCISE 1

Increasing Your Powers of Focus and Concentration

Benefit: All of us suffer from the ill effects of overstimulation in today's world. We're bombarded by information and overwhelmed by stress and find it increasingly difficult to concentrate on one thing at a time. But by performing this exercise daily over a period of two to three weeks, you will notice a dramatic improvement in your mind's ability to focus. Think of this exercise as adding a "zoom lens" to your brain—a technique that will help you immeasurably in your job, as you'll be able to keep your mind on your work for longer periods of time without becoming bored, distracted, or vulnerable to external stimuli.

Time: 5 minutes the first week, 6 minutes the second week, and so on until you reach 8–10 minutes. This exercise can be done at any time of day, in the home or at the office.

Equipment Needed: Kitchen timer or alarm clock, and a small object that fits in your hand (a pen, quarter, salt shaker, ring, etc.).

Body Position: Sitting is best, but any position will do, as long as you are comfortable and won't be distracted by noise or by having to move once you begin the exercise.

* * *

Step 1: Set a kitchen timer or alarm clock to 5 minutes and place it within hearing range. (Remember, in following weeks you will increase the length of time.)

Step 2: Place the small object in front of you or hold it with both hands.

Step 3: Begin to describe out loud *anything and everything* you notice about the object, right down to the smallest detail. ("This salt shaker is approximately 3½ inches tall. On top is a silver metal cap that has five sides. On one side there's a scratch, about one-half inch wide . . . ") Describe all shades of color on the object, as well as its texture, height, weight, and shape. Don't miss anything! Think of your eyes as zoom lenses and zoom into the smallest detail. Don't turn the object around or upside down until you have methodically described virtually everything you can see on that side.

Step 4: Continue the exercise until the timer rings. You will

now have more than enough focus power to concentrate on any project or business plan.

Note: A side benefit of this exercise is an increased level of calmness and relaxation.

WORKPLACE EXERCISE 2

Developing Mental Stamina

Benefit: Like it or not, we are required by our jobs to produce at consistently high levels—all day, all week—even when we're not feeling the least bit productive or energetic. Some of us are "morning people" who produce our best work early in the day, only to cave in as the workday comes to a close; others of us are hopeless in the morning and only come alive in the afternoon hours. Many of my clients say they often experience this high-followed-by-a-low cycle of productivity, and they've asked me for a strategy for keeping their mental output consistent during the day. After all, supervisors don't have much sympathy for the mid-morning slump, the full-stomach-after-lunch syndrome, or the late-afternoon blood-sugar low! This exercise will help you develop mental stamina on the job by tapping into a continual source of energy.

Time: 5–10 minutes whenever you feel your mental energy sagging.

Body Position: Sitting comfortably.

* * *

Step 1: Shut the door to your office and sit comfortably at your desk, or find an empty conference room and sit there. Take five deep breaths (inhale slowly through your nose, hold for 5 seconds, and exhale slowly through your mouth).

Step 2: Close your eyes and keep them closed for the remainder of the exercise. Think the word "tree." Now imagine that you are an enormous, sturdy tree (redwood, oak, or elm). Imagine that your feet and toes are your roots, your torso is your trunk, and your arms and hands are your branches. Just as a tree is connected to the earth through its roots, imagine that you are connected to the earth through your roots, which extend from your feet and toes deep into the ground, where they branch out in many directions. If possible, slip off your shoes and wiggle your toes a bit as you imagine that you're planting your roots even deeper.

Step 3: Now take ten deep breaths (inhale through your nose, hold for 5 seconds, exhale through your mouth). Each time you inhale, imagine that your roots are *pulling in* energy in the form of green nutrients from the earth's soil. Let the energy from these green nutrients travel up from your toes and feet, through all parts of your torso, out to your hands and arms, all the way up to the top of your head. Hold this energy for 5 seconds as you hold your breath. Then, as you exhale, imagine that you are *expelling* mental and physical fatigue.

Step 4: You are going to take another ten deep breaths now, but before doing so, imagine that the earth (the ground beneath you) has just received an abundant rainfall. Each time you inhale, imagine that your roots are *pulling in* energy in the form of fresh, clean water. Let the energy from its nutrients travel up from your toes and feet, through all parts of your torso, out to your hands and arms, all the way up to the top of your head. Hold this energy for 5 seconds as you hold your breath. Then, as you exhale, imagine that you are *expelling* mental and physical fatigue.

Step 5: You are going to take your final ten deep breaths now, but first, imagine that it's a brilliant, sunny day and the sun's golden rays are being absorbed by the ground beneath you. Each time you inhale, imagine that your roots are *pulling in* the energy of the bright golden sunbeams. Let the energy from these golden sunbeams travel up from your toes and feet, through all parts of your torso, out to your hands and arms, all the way up to the top of your head. Hold this energy for 5 seconds as you hold your breath. Then, as you exhale, imagine that you are *expelling* mental and physical fatigue.

Step 6: After you exhale for the last time, gently open your eyes. Get up and stretch.

Note: If you've never tried the technique of "imagining" or think you wouldn't be very good at it, *don't* pass up this exercise. Even if you don't "get into" the tree imagery, you'll be surprised how cleansed and energized you'll feel, simply by breathing deeply over the course of the exercise. Of course, the more vividly you can imagine yourself as a tree, the more you will benefit from the exercise.

Workplace Exercise 3

Asking for a Raise or Promotion

Benefit: It's amazing how many of my clients fret over the issue of asking for recognition on the job. "My boss will think I'm pushy if I ask for a raise." "I wouldn't know how to broach the subject." "Maybe I don't really deserve a promotion anyway." I hear such sentences all too often. The problem is common because most of us have been brought up to believe that modesty is the best policy. What's more, when we think about *asking* for a raise, we feel as if we're asking for a handout, which makes us feel like children approaching an authority figure for permission to do or have something. The first thing I tell my clients is: Don't imagine that you are *asking* for a raise; imagine that you are *presenting* yourself for a raise. The second thing I tell them is: Do this exercise! It won't teach you how to choose the right moment to approach your particular supervisor, nor will it teach you how to negotiate a specific salary or job title. But it will help you become comfortable with the *idea* of presenting yourself for recognition. After performing this exercise you will begin to think and feel like a confident adult who deserves his or her reward and doesn't mind asking for it—whether you're a department manager asking for advancement, a secretary needing an overdue day off, a photographer informing his clients of a fee increase, a student requesting a review of his grade, or even a husband asking his wife to praise his culinary skills.

Time: You'll need 10 minutes to prepare. The time it takes to do the actual exercise varies according to your personal needs.

Equipment Needed: Two sheets of paper and a pen.

Body Position: As the exercise dictates.

* * *

This exercise has two parts, which you will perform over a two-week period. During the first week, you will develop the habit of *rewarding* yourself. During the second week, you will develop the habit of *requesting* things from others.

Part 1 / Week 1

Step 1: Take one sheet of paper and draw a line down the center. Label the left-hand column "Reward" and the right-hand column "Justification."

Step 2: In the "Reward" column, list several rewards you'd like to give yourself this week. (I define a reward as a treat—something you want but don't normally give yourself.) Try to list at least fourteen rewards so that you can give yourself two per day for seven days. (Don't worry if you can't think of fourteen—as the week unfolds, you'll think of others.) Examples of rewards might be: "Sleep later on Saturday," "Treat myself to a homemade meal instead of takeout," "Buy that paperback novel I've been wanting to read."

Step 3: In the "Justification" column next to each reward, write a simple, logical reason why you're entitled to that reward ("I deserve to sleep late on Saturday because I haven't done it in months").

Step 4: As soon as you've completed your lists of rewards and justifications, begin giving yourself the rewards, two per day for seven days, if possible. Each time you reward yourself during the week, make a mental note of the justification. When the week is over, go on to Part 2/Week 2.

Part 2 / Week 2

Step 1: Take the other sheet of paper and print the word "Requests" at the top.

Step 2: List at least fourteen requests you'd like to make of others this week, two per day for seven days. As in Part 1, don't worry if you can't think of fourteen requests; they'll come to you as the days go by. Examples might be: "Ask my husband to pick up my clothes at the dry cleaner," "Ask my brother to help me hang pictures around my apartment," or "Ask my sister if I can borrow her necklace."

Step 3: As soon as you've completed your list of requests, begin making them at the rate of two per day for seven days, if possible.

Note: While you may not have any problem rewarding yourself, you might be uncomfortable asking things of others. If that's true for you, skip Part 1, go directly to Part 2, and perform the steps in Part 2 for *two* weeks. If you are comfortable requesting things of others but have difficulty with the idea of rewarding yourself, perform the steps in Part 1 for *two* weeks and don't bother with Part 2. The point here is to get yourself in the habit of believing you deserve rewards, whether you give them to yourself or request them from others.

WORKPLACE EXERCISE 4

Avoiding Friction With Coworkers

Benefit: "If there's more than one person in a room, there's bound to be a clash." That old saying isn't far from the truth. Every office environment comes with its own peculiar interaction of personalities—the overachiever, the underachiever, the imperious boss, and the whiny underling all have to work together. Inevitably, tempers flare, frustrations fester, and jealousies boil over, all at the same time you're expected to perform at peak level. When my clients complain about supervisors, coworkers, and subordinates who annoy them, I explain that working with difficult colleagues needn't give them ulcers, or worse, force them to find work elsewhere.

What's the solution? Learning how to train your mind to break the cause-and-effect cycle that underlies these emotionally charged relationships. Here are some typical examples of causes for annoyance: "Leonard calls those early morning meetings and then shows up late—just to prove who's boss." "I send a proposal to my manager and he nitpicks it to death." These causes stem from quirks in the coworker's personality and are, therefore, *out* of your control. But the ways you're *affected* by the coworker are entirely *within* your control.

This exercise brings to an abrupt halt that negative cycle of cause and effect. Originally, I created it for my professional athlete clients, who kept complaining that bad calls, crowd noise, and cheating opponents were preventing them from playing their best. Later, I offered the exercise to my business clients, who report the same positive results the athletes discovered.

Time: 1–2 minutes preparation time and 1–5 minutes performance time.

Equipment Needed: Pen and paper (optional).

Body Position: As the exercise dictates.

*   *   *

Step 1: *Preparation.* This exercise calls for a series of quick mental commands. Once you begin, don't stop or let anything interrupt you. With practice, it will only take you 1–3 minutes to perform. The command words are: *stop, cancel, release, relax, refocus.* If you choose, take a sheet of paper and print these words in large block letters. Place the sheet on your desk or in a drawer, someplace to which you have easy access. Hang on to the sheet until you know the sequence of the commands by heart.

Step 2: The next time a coworker behaves in a way that annoys, frustrates, or upsets you, immediately command your mind to *stop*. (*Stop* means: "I am going to *stop* any further effect his behavior has on me right now!")

Step 3: Then command your mind to *cancel*. (*Cancel* means: "I am canceling any negative feeling I have toward this person at this moment.")

Step 4: Then command your mind to *release*. (*Release* means: "I'm completely releasing any negative feeling from my body right now.") Snap your fingers, crack your knuckles, or clear your throat as a physical cue.

Step 5: Now command your mind to *relax*. (*Relax* means: "I am relaxing myself at this moment by taking three deep breaths.") Take three deep breaths.

Step 6: Command your mind to *refocus*. (*Refocus* means: "I am refocusing my mind on my work."

Note: If you are still feeling frustrated after performing this exercise, repeat STEPS 4 and 5, this time executing STEP 4 in the following manner: Instead of simply commanding your mind to *release*, issue a separate command to the specific parts of your body that are tight with tension ("Neck *release!*" "Chest *release!*" "Stomach *release!*" and so on, right down to "Toes *release!*"). Focusing on a specific body part is another way of employing a physical cue as a means of relieving frustration or stress. When you watch a televised sporting event and see an athlete make a fist, yell, or slap his thigh, you're observing the athlete perform a version of this sequence of mental commands. His goal is to pull his focus immediately back to winning the next point, in spite of the annoyance that has distracted him. That's what this exercise will do for you—enable you to pull your focus *away* from the annoying colleague and the effect he's had on you and *toward* the business at hand.

WORKPLACE EXERCISE 5

Conquering Public Speaking Jitters

Benefit: As many readers know, one of the most common fears plaguing men and women of all ages is the fear of public speaking. More than 70 percent of us experience real terror when faced with the prospect of addressing an audience—whether the audience is a conference room full of coworkers or a ballroom filled with conventioneers. The cause of public speaking jitters isn't hard to figure out: We get anxious when we focus, not on the material we're presenting, but on the ways the audience will scrutinize and judge our performance.

How can we conquer our fear of public speaking? Some speakers think that if they could only cling to their lectern or hold on to their index cards for dear life, they'd feel more "grounded" during their presentation. But clutching physical objects with a death grip won't exactly go unnoticed by the audience, the very group they're trying so hard to impress. So I've devised a grounding technique that accomplishes the same goal. It uses a concept called "finding the horizon," which means lifting your focus from the anxiety inside you to a specific visual point in the audience (the horizon) and holding it there in order to keep your emotions *level*. Have you ever been in the cockpit of an airplane and seen the instrument pilots refer to as the artificial horizon? It looks something like this:

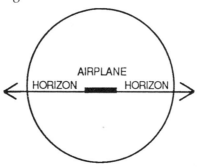

In the above diagram, the plane is not flying level to the earth's horizon, so the pilot must turn the plane and right the wings until the line that represents "airplane" is level with the lines that represent "horizon," as in the diagram below.

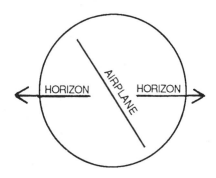

This exercise teaches you how to find and focus on your horizon when you speak in public, to right yourself when you feel fearful, and to ground yourself by giving you something to hold on to. It's simple to do—no one in the audience will notice—and you'll "fly" through your performance steady and sure.

Time: 5–10 minutes for preparation; then use the technique while speaking in public.

Equipment Needed: None.

Body Position: Standing.

* * *

Step 1: The next time you're called upon to speak in front of a group, do this simple preparation once a day for three to five days prior to your speaking engagement. Stand in a room and face any wall. Look straight ahead at the wall and focus your eyes on a visual point, preferably at eye level (a painting, window, bookcase, etc.). In your mind's eye, draw an imaginary horizontal line through that visual point (for example, draw an imaginary horizontal line through a painting, as pictured below). This will be your horizon.

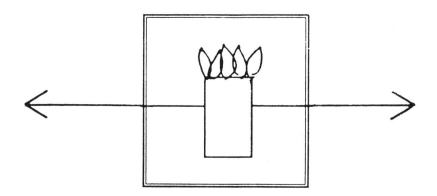

Step 2: For the next 5 minutes or so, speak out loud about any subject that comes to mind. (If you can recite parts of your speech, so much the better.) As you speak, make sure you continue to make eye contact with your imaginary horizon. Your eyes may move to the right or left as you speak, but your vision must never veer off the horizontal line.

Step 3: In this preparatory step, you will practice moving your line of vision back and forth from your horizon to notes or index cards in your hands. (If you won't be referring to printed material during your presentation, skip this step and go on to the next.) Over the next 5 minutes, read from your notes or index cards, glance up, find your horizon, and continue speaking. Remember: Once you've located your horizon, your eyes may move from left to right or right to left as long as they *stay* on the line. Go back and forth from your notes to your horizon and continue speaking.

Step 4: Now you're ready to appear before a live audience! As soon as you stand up to speak (if you're sitting, the same process applies), choose a horizon point in the audience. My favorite horizon point is a straight line across the eyes of one of the audience members, as shown below. Remember: Don't look *into* the person's eyes; look at the line that runs *across* them.

As you speak, *speak directly to this line.* If you must direct your comments to one decision maker, as you would during a presentation to an important client, simply position your horizon point along the straight line through the middle of his or her eyes and allow your eyes to travel back and forth from one of his eyes to the other.

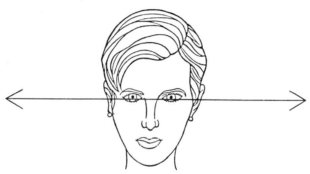

Step 5: If you need to refer to notes or pause for a sip of water, do so and then return your gaze to your horizon, just as you did in STEP 3. Your mind will be so "busy" finding and staying on your horizon that it won't have any energy left for feeling anxious. If, however, you do experience some nervousness during your presentation, blink your eyes as a physical cue, reminding yourself to refocus on your horizon. Nervousness will only creep into your mind when you've let yourself look into an audience member's eyes instead of looking at the horizontal line that runs through them. The point isn't to get you caught up in what he's thinking; it's to get him caught up in what you're saying!

WORKPLACE EXERCISE 6

Becoming a More Creative Thinker

Benefit: Do you envy coworkers who always seem to come up with fresh, innovative ideas while *you're* stuck in the same old thought patterns? Have you ever wondered why your own "creative juices" stopped flowing? Do you wish you could rekindle the spark but don't know how? Many of my clients lament their lack of creativity on the job, particularly with the ruthless demands of today's professional marketplace, where you're only as good as your last deal and you're expected to create on demand—yesterday! Take heart, though, because heightening your powers of creativity has less to do with the pressures of your specific profession and more to do with getting your mind to produce *new and different signals*, which is what this exercise will teach you to do. How? First, you must recognize that your mind has gotten used to sorting and cataloging millions of bits of information over the years and then feeding you those bits of data when you need them. What's more, there are noticeable *themes and patterns* to your sorting and cataloging—and it's these very themes and patterns that must be broken in order to increase creativity. To do this, you must "confuse" the mind and force it to reprogram how it takes in and records information. Once you've broken your worn-out thought patterns, or mindsets, your mind will begin to sort and catalog information in new ways—and then fresh, new ideas will be born! This mental exercise trains you to break mind-sets. Unlike other exercises in this chapter, this one doesn't stress the importance of focus and concentration. In fact, *don't* concentrate at all while you're doing it! Simply go through the motions as I describe them, without giving much thought to the changes your mind is undergoing. After performing the exercise for two to three weeks, you'll be amazed at the new ideas that will start popping into your mind.

Time: Throughout the day. Each activity will take 1–5 minutes.

Equipment Needed: None.

Body Position: As the exercise dictates.

* * *

Step 1: There are no sequential "steps" for you to take, just activities to perform—activities that make up your normal daily routine. But I'm going to ask you to do them differently in order to "confuse" your mind and break old thought patterns. Following is a sample schedule for three days' worth of activities. Try to do *at least* one activity per day. But for best results, do three per day, as in the sample schedule, and continue mixing up your routine for two to three weeks. Once you get the hang of this exercise you can add activities of your own.

Monday

1. Brush your teeth with the opposite hand (if you're right-handed, brush with your left hand, and vice versa).

2. Sit in a different chair at the dining room table.

3. Sleep on the opposite side of the bed (or sleep in a different room).

Tuesday
(Keep performing the previous day's activities.)

1. Read your *least* favorite section of the newspaper first.

2. Drink all beverages with the opposite hand.

3. Move articles on your desk to a different part of your office (in-box or Rolodex) so that you have to get up and walk across the room each time you use them.

Wednesday
(Keep performing the previous days' activities.)

1. Wear your watch on the opposite wrist.

2. Take a different route to work. (If there's only one expressway or subway line, simply circle the parking lot twice before parking or walk around the building twice before entering.)

Note: It's okay if you forget to perform an activity or two from the previous day. Just try to do *as many things differently* as you can over the course of two or three weeks. Sure, you'll feel slightly disoriented, but that's the point of this exercise. It's the disorientation that eventually leads to creativity. A similar process takes place when you return home from a vacation. While you were away, your mind was forced to rearrange its patterns. As a result, it saw things differently and you came home feeling renewed, refreshed, and open to new ideas. If you continue to rearrange your thought patterns for two to three weeks while performing this exercise, you'll be surprised how renewed, refreshed, and open to new ideas you'll feel, once the initial feelings of confusion and disorientation dissipate. One word of caution, though: Never do an activity that may endanger your safety—like operating a power saw with your weaker hand!

WORKPLACE EXERCISE 7

Achieving Championship-Level Thinking

Benefit: What makes a champion? (1) Talent. (2) The discipline required to perfect that talent. (3) Something I call "championship-level thinking," which is the ability to raise the level of your performance by focusing on a goal and making it your personal mission to attain that goal. Championship-level thinking involves selecting a thought or phrase and repeatedly registering and recording it in your mind, so that it becomes your "theme." (This thought process is also known as "Destination/Target" thinking.) The champions I know—whether they're top tennis players or successful business executives—practice Destination/Target thinking *naturally*. They're able to have a clear mental picture of their destination, which might be an upcoming tennis tournament, an important history exam, or a year-end sales report, as well as a clear mental picture of their target, which might be getting to the finals of the tennis tournament, scoring an A on the history test, or bringing in a $50,000 increase in sales. Champions are able to fix these Destination/Target images in their minds by focusing on them for a few minutes each day—that's *why* they're consistently outpacing their competition! This exercise will give *you* a chance to think like a champion. It might seem too simple to work, but—believe me—it does! However, because this exercise requires a considerable amount of focus power, I recommend that you try it *after* you've spent a few days doing the exercise in this chapter called "Increasing Your Powers of Focus and Concentration."

Time: 5 minutes preparation time and another 10 minutes for the exercise, which may be done first thing in the morning after you've done the warm-up exercise called "Getting Your Mind in Gear" or just before going to sleep at night. See the note at the end of the following steps for further information about how and when to do this exercise.

Equipment Needed: Three sheets of light-colored construction paper (opaque), scissors, a CD, tape, or record with at least 10 minutes' worth of instrumental music, and a kitchen timer or alarm clock.

Body Position: Sitting or standing.

*   *   *

Step 1: *Preparation.* Take one sheet of construction paper and cut out a circle approximately 1½ inches in diameter in the center of the sheet. This sheet will be called your "scope." Take a second sheet of paper, print "Destination: _____" directly in the center of the sheet, and fill in your Destination or project (e.g., winter sales meeting, Boston Marathon, New York Bar exam, etc.). Take the third sheet of paper, print "Target: _____" directly in the center of the sheet, and

fill in your Target or *exact* goal or expectation you have regarding your Destination (e.g., $50,000 sales increase, 3:30 running time, passing the Bar, etc.). Your materials are now prepared.

Step 2: Hold your scope sheet approximately 2½–3 inches in front of your face, with the cutout circle at eye level. Without moving the scope, alternate closing one eye and opening the other; you'll notice that as you're looking through the scope, you're seeing a different part of the room through each eye, thereby creating two different lines of vision.

Step 3: Take your Destination and Target sheets and either

tack them up on the wall or place them on a flat surface (a table or the floor). Make sure the sheets are right in front of you in direct line with your newly created two different lines of vision. You should be able to hold your scope still and then, simply by opening and closing each eye, see a different written message, with almost everything else near your line of vision blocked out (paintings on the wall, newspapers on a table, etc.). It doesn't matter which line of vision "sees" which sheet (Destination or Target).

Step 4: Turn on the stereo and put on the instrumental music. It's up to you whether it's classical or heavy metal, as long as you find it pleasing to listen to.

Step 5: Set the timer or alarm clock for 10 minutes and place it close by, so you'll hear it ring.

Step 6: With your Destination and Target sheets already in place in their separate lines of vision, pick up your scope sheet and hold it in front of your face. Close the eye that will see "Target" and open the eye that will see "Destination." Then begin to alternate, gently opening and closing each eye after you've looked at each sheet for 5 seconds (e.g., left eye sees "Destination: winter sales meeting" for 5 seconds, right eye sees "Target: $50,000 sales increase" for 5 seconds, left eye, right eye, etc.).

Step 7: Simply read each phrase to yourself every time you see it in your line of vision. Don't add words—just read what you see.

Step 8: If your mind wanders, stop the exercise, shut both eyes, count to 5, and begin again. Remember, the goal here is to focus your mind on and record your Destination and Target phrases over and over again.

Step 9: When the timer rings, shut both eyes, count to 10, and open them.

Note: This exercise works best when the goals you're asking your mind to record are clearly defined and described, as opposed to goals of a general nature, such as "I want to be happy." If possible, start performing the exercise thirty days prior to your actual Destination. If you have a long-term goal in mind (perhaps a project that won't begin for several months), so much the better. The longer your mind has to receive and record your phrases of intent, the more effective this exercise will be. If, however, your project is only a few weeks away, simply do this exercise more than once a day.

3

Exercises for Romantic Relationships

A few years ago, I saw a television program about a husband and wife of the "thirtysomething" generation who were desperately trying to keep their romance alive amid the pressures of work, kids, and changing feelings toward each other. "Why are we going through this when we were supposed to be so happy?" the wife wailed. By the end of the show, the couple figured out that they were having problems in their marriage because their parents had fed them unrealistic expectations of what love and marriage were all about. "Maybe we just expect too much," the husband concluded.

I chuckled when I heard that line, because it's a line I've heard all too often from my clients, most of whom were raised with similarly unrealistic expectations.

Having a healthy, enduring love relationship is difficult at best, but now couples face graver challenges—challenges their parents never dreamed of—from sexually transmitted diseases to divorce and single parenting. What are men and women of the nineties to do? They *want* to be in a loving relationship, but they want to do it *better* than they did it in high school and college, *better* than they did it in their first marriage, *better* than their parents did it. But before they

37

know it, their unrealistic expectations are making a difficult situation even more difficult.

I don't mean to suggest that I don't approve of couples who want their love relationship to be blissful—on the contrary! There's nothing more satisfying than building a sound, healthy relationship. But working on a relationship—really working—requires mental fitness and stamina. It's up to each partner to take responsibility for his part in the partnership, whether that means learning how to control anger or knowing how to rekindle feelings of passion.

The exercises in this chapter are geared for men and women who want to be in a healthy, loving relationship and are willing to work toward that goal. The exercises needn't be used by both partners in the relationship, although *two* mentally fit partners are certainly better than *one*. Often, it only takes one partner to raise the relationship to a more positive level. Remember: You'll be in a much better position to encourage your partner to pursue a program of mental fitness if *you* seem happier, calmer, more mentally fit.

Several of the exercises in this chapter are relevant to other aspects of daily life. "Easing Dating Jitters" can be used to alleviate all kind of social jitters. "Repairing Self-Esteem After Rejection" will help anyone suffering the sting of rejection, whether in the workplace or in a friendship. "Refocusing on Your Partner's Positive Attributes" isn't just applicable for lovers; it's a great exercise to do if you're having negative thoughts about your parents, friends, or coworkers. "Releasing Anger Constructively" is effective for any situation in which you need to regain control over your emotions. And "Staying Within Yourself" offers quick relief for anyone who feels he's being manipulated, whether by a romantic partner, a demanding boss, or a needy friend.

Romantic Relationship Exercise 1

Easing Dating Anxiety

Benefit: Almost all of my clients experience some form of anxiety when meeting new people—anxiety ranging from stomach "butterflies" to full-blown avoidance of social functions. We're a nation of people known for our aggressiveness, yet we're often self-conscious when we're face to face with a new person. The causes of this anxiety aren't very mysterious, though; they're triggered by our wondering and worrying how we'll look, talk, and act, not to mention how the other person will look, talk, and act. But an encounter with a new person needn't be stressful if we recognize and focus on the *structure* each encounter follows. By structure I mean that, just like a three-act play, each interaction with a new person breaks down into three parts—the Beginning, Middle, and End. By directing our minds back to this mental "map" during a social encounter instead of dwelling on negative, anxiety-producing thoughts about ourselves or the encounter, we can ease and even eliminate the anxiety, no matter how long the encounter lasts. As simple as it sounds, if we just repeat the words "Beginning," "Middle," and "End" whenever our focus drifts back to such thoughts as "I wonder if I'm talking too fast" or "Am I revealing too much?" our concerns about how we'll be perceived or judged by others will dissipate.

Time: 1–5 minutes.

Equipment Needed: None.

Body Position: As the exercise dictates.

* * *

Step 1: Prepare for your date or meeting with the new person by mentally reviewing the following three parts of an encounter:

A. The Beginning: We'll exchange names and superficial references about ourselves.
B. The Middle: We'll reveal stories, information, experiences, opinions, or feelings to each other.
C. The End: We'll conclude the encounter with some form of goodbye.

It's not necessary to memorize the descriptions of the three parts, as long as you have a general understanding of the *structure* the encounter follows. You should, however, memorize the three reference words: "Beginning," "Middle," and "End."

Step 2: Your trigger to start this exercise is the *moment* you experience anxiety during the encounter. Say to yourself, "Stop! Which part am I in?" If you're in the Beginning of the encounter, say the word "Beginning" to yourself several times until the anxiety dissipates. You will be able to converse with the person at the same time as you are repeating the word "Beginning" to yourself.

Step 3: If you find that the encounter with the new person gets off to an anxiety-free start but that anxiety creeps in as the conversation moves from superficial to more revealing, use the anxiety to trigger the exercise. Say to yourself, "Stop! Which part am I in?" Then, as the conversation continues, say the word "Middle" to yourself several times until the anxiety dissipates.

Step 4: If you've felt relaxed during the entire encounter but begin to experience anxiety as the meeting winds down, use the anxiety to trigger the exercise. Say to yourself, "Stop! Which part am I in?" Then, as the encounter concludes, say the word "End" to yourself several times.

Note: You can perform this exercise during the entire encounter, no matter how long the encounter lasts. You will find, however, that you'll only have to repeat your reference words for a minute or so for the anxiety to subside. If you're wondering how in the world you'll be able to say these words in your head while carrying on a coherent conversation with the new person, guess what: You do this all the time. The next time you talk to a friend or coworker face-to-face, notice how your thoughts wander—to her clothes, to his cologne, to your next meal, etc. The mind is incredibly acrobatic and can juggle two thoughts at once.

ROMANTIC RELATIONSHIP EXERCISE 2

Repairing Self-Esteem After Rejection

Benefit: Everyone strives for intimacy and closeness in their loving relationships. But there's a risk to intimacy and closeness: rejection! Whether it rears its ugly head during a marital rift or the breakup of a business partnership, rejection hurts—badly—and it carries with it a poison that can eat away at your self-esteem. More specifically, when somebody rejects you, you feel pain; then you begin to view yourself in a negative light; then you denigrate yourself with such thoughts as "Something must be wrong with me" or "If I were smarter, richer, and better-looking, she wouldn't have rejected me"; then, before you know it, your self-esteem has been destroyed. This exercise is designed to interrupt the dangerous cycle of rejection-pain-negativity before it erodes your self-esteem completely. Think of it as an emergency approach. It's not intended to help you repair a relationship, nor is it designed to help you understand why the relationship failed (only after the pain of rejection has lessened can you begin to analyze the situation and make rational decisions about it). It *is* designed to *snap* you out of your negative thoughts before they threaten to destroy the positive self-image you have spent years trying to achieve. How does it work? It uses a "physical cue" to change your mental outlook and forces you to interrupt your thoughts of rejection and the accompanying feelings of despondency and refocus on more positive self-talk. Behavioral psychologists often use physical or mental "cues" to trigger positive thoughts and behaviors in their clients. For this exercise, I've created a rather intense physical cue—snapping a rubber band against your wrist—to trigger positive thoughts and behaviors in people who've suffered a loss of self-esteem due to a rejection. The slight stinging sensation you will feel after snapping the rubber band against your wrist is just harsh enough to get your attention off your feelings of despair and snap you back to more positive self-talk. Yes, the exercise may cause you some discomfort, but it's guaranteed to call a halt to the stream of negative, self-defeating thoughts rolling around in your head. Every time you snap the rubber band against your wrist and feel the sting, you'll think, "Whoa! Why am I hurting myself with these awful, self-destructive thoughts? Enough is enough!"

Time: 1–3 minutes throughout the day.

Equipment Needed: One rubber band large enough to wear on your wrist comfortably without pinching.

Body Position: As the exercise dictates.

*   *   *

Step 1: To give you an idea of how this exercise works, put a rubber band on one of your wrists as if it were a watchband. Now pull it back a little and let it snap with enough force to draw your focus to the sight and sound of the snapping. (The snapping is your physical cue.)

Step 2: The next time you feel rejected, sad, hurt, depressed, or just down on yourself emotionally, put on your rubber wristband. As you're about to think negative thoughts or replay the rejection scene in your mind, *stop* whatever you're doing and *snap* the rubber band against your wrist several times.

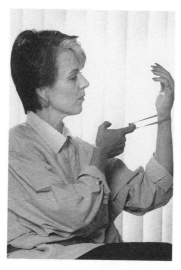

Step 3: Each time you hear the snap and feel the slight sting, repeat a positive message about yourself—a phrase that's intended to bolster your sagging self-esteem ("I'm a valuable person who has a lot to offer" or "I love and appreciate myself and can weather this difficult situation").

Step 4: Repeat STEP 3 throughout a particularly tough day or evening or whenever you sense your thoughts and feelings drifting over to memories of the rejection. If you're at a social function where it would be inappropriate to wear the rubber band, simply pinch yourself several times on the wrist and repeat STEP 3.

Step 5: Continue to perform this exercise for several hours or days, until you feel that you've overcome the worst of the trauma.

Note: You may change your phrase or positive message each time you do the exercise. Just make sure it's a phrase that's entirely positive in tone and substance and makes you feel more upbeat and at peace with yourself.

ROMANTIC RELATIONSHIP EXERCISE 3

Rekindling Feelings of Passion

Benefit: At one time or another, virtually all of my clients have reported that they've lost their desire for sex—that they're too busy or too stressed out or too worried about their performance to feel passionate about themselves and, therefore, their partners. Since I believe that feelings of passion and sexuality originate in the mind, I created this mental exercise to help "program" the mind for passion and love-making. The hardest part of this exercise will be to give yourself permission to do it. What you do with your partner *after* performing this exercise is up to you. The exercise is merely a way of "getting you in the mood" for passion. Its goal is to *lock* your mind into an attractive, playful, uninhibited image of yourself.

Time: 10–15 minutes any time of day or night.

Equipment Needed: A watch with a second hand, a blank piece of paper, and a pen.

Body Position: Sitting or reclining.

*   *   *

Step 1: In the center of a blank piece of paper, write your first name. (See illustration 1.) Now draw four lines leading from your name to the top, sides, and bottom of the paper. (See illustration 2.) Set the pen and paper aside.

Step 2: Sitting or lying down comfortably, take the watch in both hands and hold it close enough to your eyes for you to see the second hand sweep around. For 5 minutes (five times around the face of the watch), simply watch the second hand move, counting the minutes and seconds as you go. It will get cumbersome to count, "1 minute 2," "1 minute 3," so just abbreviate and say, "1–2, 1–3, 1–4," etc.

Step 3: After the 5 minutes are up, gently close your eyes and think or say out loud the words "safe and secure." Then envision any situation/person/place/object that elicits feelings of safety and security (e.g., wrapping yourself in an old down quilt, sitting by a roaring fire, spending an afternoon with a trusted friend, etc.). Say to yourself, "This thought of feeling safe and secure is now locked into my brain on the count of 10." Then count to 10.

Step 4: Think or say out loud the words "sexy and attractive." Then envision any situation/person/place/object that elicits feelings of sexuality and attractiveness (e.g., an article of clothing you own or saw in a magazine, a chance encounter with an old love, a scene from an erotic book or film, etc.). Say to yourself, "This thought or memory of feeling sexy and attractive is now locked into my brain on the count of 10." Then count to 10.

Step 5: Think or say out loud the word "uninhibited." Then envision any situation/person/place/object that elicits feelings of openness, relaxation, freedom, and lack of inhibition. If you don't have an actual memory of feeling uninhibited, create a thought or situation with you as the star (e.g., you're standing at the center of a concert stage and belting out a tune in front of hundreds of people). Say to yourself, "This thought or memory of feeling uninhibited is now locked into my brain on the count of 10." Then count to 10.

Step 6: Think or say out loud the word "playful." Proceed as with the above steps, envisioning scenes where you were allowed to be playful, silly, funny, or even childish. When you've selected your scene, say to yourself, "This thought or memory of feeling playful is now locked into my brain on the count of 10." Then count to 10.

Step 7: Gently open your eyes. Pick up the pen and sheet of paper. At the top of the page, write the words *safe and secure.* (See illustration 3.) To the right, write the words *sexy and*

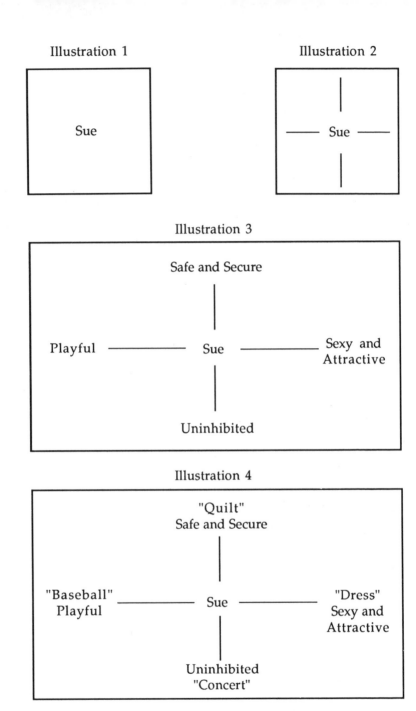

Illustration 1

Sue

Illustration 2

Sue

Illustration 3

Safe and Secure

Playful ——————— Sue ——————— Sexy and Attractive

Uninhibited

Illustration 4

"Quilt" Safe and Secure

"Baseball" Playful ——————— Sue ——————— "Dress" Sexy and Attractive

Uninhibited "Concert"

attractive. At the bottom, write the word *uninhibited*. To the left, write the word *playful*.

Step 8: Above the words *safe and secure* (see illustration 4), write a one-word label taken from the thought or memory that made you feel safe and secure (e.g., *quilt*).To the right of the words *sexy and attractive*, write a one-word label taken from the thought or memory that made you feel sexy and attractive. Underneath the word *uninhibited*, write a one-word label taken from the thought or memory that made you feel uninhibited. To the left of the word *playful*, write a one-word label taken from the thought or memory that made you feel playful.

Step 9: Holding the sheet of paper in front of you, focus your eyes on your one-word label above the words *safe and secure*. Simply look at the word and count to 15. Then move your eyes clockwise around the paper and focus on your one-word label to the right of the words *sexy and attractive*. Look at the word and count to 15. Continue moving clockwise around the paper until you have focused on each one-word label for 15 seconds. Then repeat the entire procedure five times.

Step 10: You have now locked a mental image of a more passionate, sexy version of you into your brain with word cues. Refer to this sheet of paper whenever you want to "get back into the mood" or rekindle feelings of passion.

ROMANTIC RELATIONSHIP EXERCISE 4

Refocusing on Your Partner's Positive Attributes

Benefit: What's that old saying? "Your partner hasn't changed . . . you're just finally seeing him as he really is!" If you're in an important, committed relationship—whether marital, live-in, or exclusive dating—you've probably experienced those rocky periods when your partner just can't seem to do anything right in your eyes. During those bleak times, it's hard to remember the early days of your courtship when all you saw was your partner's good qualities. Inevitably, time and real life begin to chip away at the concept of "partner perfection" until you're stuck with its flip side: "partner inadequacy." Why? Because sharing *any* form of emotional or physical space with someone involves negotiation, compromise, forgiveness, trust, perseverance, and just plain hard work. Before you know it, you're no longer seeing your partner through rose-colored glasses. This exercise is designed to help you get back the loving, positive feelings you had toward your partner when you first met. It is *not* designed to treat serious problems, nor is it intended as a substitute for marriage counseling. What it *is* designed to do is show you how to see your partner in a positive light, as opposed to a negative one. It's designed to help you refocus on the "whole" of your partner, instead of dwelling on their individual shortcomings. And once your partner feels loved and accepted again, they'll be able to refocus their feelings on *your* positive attributes. To sum up, this mental exercise will get you in shape to focus on what's *right* about your partner, not what's wrong.

Time: 10–15 minutes, any time of day or night.

Equipment Needed: Pencil, two sheets of paper, and a snapshot of your partner, if you have one.

Body Position: Any position in which you can write comfortably.

* * *

Step 1: Write your partner's name in big letters at the top of two blank sheets of paper.

Step 2: Since the point of this exercise is to eliminate your negative feelings toward your partner, you're going to focus on them first. On one sheet of paper, list as succinctly as possible all the things about your partner that disturb you (e.g., #1 "He's selfish"; #2 "She nags"; #3 "He won't lend a hand around the house," and so on). Keep adding to the list until you run out of shortcomings. Then put the sheet aside and go on to the next step.

Step 3: Go down your list of complaints. After you read the first complaint, close your eyes and spend a few minutes imagining that you are telling your partner how you feel when he or she exhibits this behavior. "Talk" to him as if he were in the room with you. Tell him how you'd prefer him to act the next time. Be specific; offer examples. When you feel you've "vented" enough on this complaint or shortcoming, open your eyes and read the next complaint. Work your way down the list in this manner. Then proceed to STEP 4.

Step 4: Stand up and take a few minutes to clear out the negative thoughts and feelings you've just brought to the surface (water the plants, get a cup of coffee, etc.).

Step 5: Place the snapshot of your partner in front of you and stare at it for a few minutes. Then take the other sheet of paper with your partner's name at the top, and stare at it. (If you don't have a photo of your partner, just stare at his name on the sheet of paper.)

Step 6: On that sheet of paper, list as succinctly as possible instances where your partner demonstrated the *opposite* behavior from that which you described on your sheet of complaints (e.g., #1 "He's selfish" becomes #1 "He lent me his car"; #2 "She nags" becomes #2 "She didn't say anything when I ruined dinner"; #3 "He doesn't lend a hand around the house" becomes #3 "He helped clean the carpet"). The point here is to *stretch* your memory to recall the positive sides of your partner. If you're thinking, "I can't do this step because my partner never does anything I want him to," go back to STEP 3 and take a mini-break. Obviously, you're stuck on proving yourself right and may need to bring a few more negative emotions to the surface. Once you're ready to get on with more positive feelings, return to this step.

Step 7: Stare directly at your partner's face in the photo (or at his name on the paper) and imagine that you're telling him how you feel when he exhibits these positive attributes. Think about how good it is to have harmony between the two of you. Tell yourself that it's completely within your control to bring out these good, positive feelings, as *you* are the one who will decide which "picture" of your partner you will carry around all day.

Step 8: Fold the sheet of paper listing your partner's positive attributes and place it in your wallet or purse. If you feel yourself slipping into a negative mind-set during the day, reread what we'll call your "positive focus crib sheet." If possible, carry the snapshot and crib sheet together.

Note: Perform this exercise whenever you feel your partner's shortcomings piling up in your mind. Or do it when there's only one shortcoming that's bugging you. Just make sure you *don't* skip the step in which you release your negative emotions—it's an important part of the exercise. If you don't deal with your negative thoughts and feelings toward your partner, they'll fester and grow, which is damaging to any relationship.

ROMANTIC RELATIONSHIP EXERCISE 5

Releasing Anger Constructively

Benefit: Have you every been so angry at your partner that you felt as if you might explode? Have you ever unleashed this rage upon your partner, only to feel remorse later? Have you ever attacked your partner so forcefully that it took days or even weeks for his or her emotional wound to heal? Have you ever lashed out so irrationally that the relationship actually fell apart as a result? Chances are, you've answered "yes" to at least one of these questions, because people in relationships *do* get angry at each other—it's inevitable. What *doesn't* have to be inevitable is the breakup of the relationship. It's not anger that destroys marriages; it's what you do with the anger that causes irreparable damage. This exercise will help you handle your anger by cutting it down to a manageable level. It will not teach you how to repress your anger, which only wreaks havoc on the body by triggering a host of physical ills. It will show you how to release your anger, control it, and express it calmly to your partner. It will coach you on sharing your angry feelings with your mate without firing verbal bullets. It is designed for people who truly want to keep their relationships going and are, therefore, willing to assume responsibility for their anger. It's for people who are looking for a safe, effective way to vent their rage without dealing their relationship a fatal blow.

Time: 10–20 minutes.

Equipment Needed: Flashlight.

Body Position: Sitting.

*   *   *

Step 1: Find a room large enough for you to be able to sit 10–15 feet away from one of the walls. Shut off all lights and close all doors and drapes in order to make the room as dark as possible.

Step 2: Choose a wall with a bare spot (no pictures, book-shelves, windows, etc.) of at least 3 feet in diameter. Sit facing the wall, 1–2 feet away. Turn on your flashlight and aim it directly at the bare spot on the wall. The beam of light should be rather intense at such close range, and its circle of light should be very defined.

Step 3: Think of this intense circle of light as the spot where you're going to *focus* and *release* all of your anger. Either out loud or to yourself, describe anything and everything you're angry about. Don't edit or censor your feelings. Imagine that your anger is traveling a direct path, from inside your gut, down into the hand that's holding the flashlight, and out through the beam of light. As this beam of light hits the spot on the wall, imagine that your anger is as intense as the light itself.

Step 4: Take as much time as you need to express your anger. When the intensity of your feelings begins to subside, get up and move back another 2–3 feet from the wall. Sit down again, face the wall, and aim the flashlight at it. You'll notice that the circle of light is a bit larger but weaker and less defined.

Step 5: Continue to release your angry thoughts and feelings. Like the circle of light, these thoughts and feelings will become a little less intense as you begin to get in touch with the hurt that underlies your anger. Describe these hurt feelings, direct them at the circle of light, and allow them to be absorbed into the wall. Take as much time as you need to express your hurt. If your feelings of rage return, repeat STEPS 3 and 4.

Step 6: After several minutes, get up and move back another 2–3 feet from the wall. Sit down again, face the wall, and aim your flashlight at it. By now the beam of light and the circle it creates are quite diffuse. This weaker light represents your newly diffused angry feelings. Begin to express your thoughts now, describing why you were angry in the first place. Make your sentences clear and calm in tone, and observe how you've been able to control and manage your rage. After several minutes, shut off the flashlight, close your eyes, and spend a few minutes in total silence. Then get up, turn on lights, open drapes, and leave the room. Remind yourself that your anger has been released and absorbed by the circle of light. Those thoughts which you expressed while facing the weakest, most diffuse circle of light are the thoughts you will now be able to communicate to your partner.

ROMANTIC RELATIONSHIP EXERCISE 6

Staying Within Yourself

Benefit: Have you ever wanted to achieve a personal goal—lose weight, get a graduate degree, learn a new hobby, etc.—but found that your resolve wilted when your partner expressed disapproval or even disdain for your plans? Have you ever gotten up in the morning, ready to tackle the "must-do's" on your list, only to accomplish none of them, thanks to your partner's insistence that *his* or *her* needs come first? Have you ever spent hours anticipating what your partner will think about something you've done—hours that could have been much better spent improving some aspect of yourself or your environment? Have you ever felt as if your emotional well-being depended on that of your partner's?

If you've answered yes to one or all of these questions, you're not alone. Many of my clients have felt "co-dependent" with their partner, to use a popular term of the day. Obviously, when you share your life with another person, there will be times when you'll feel dependent on that person for love and support. But healthy relationships are made up of two individuals who've come to rely on themselves for a sense of self-esteem and well-being—individuals who take responsibility for their *own* happiness and don't place unreasonable demands on their partner or on the relationship. As a therapist, I try to teach clients how to maintain their self-identity while participating in a loving relationship. I try to show them that, by allowing their partner's behavior to affect theirs, or by adapting their behavior to gain their partner's approval, they lose their sense of themselves. If you're a sports fan, you know that athletes are often instructed to "play their zone" in order to defend a specific area of the playing field from attack. Perhaps you've also heard the phrase "stay within yourself" to describe the same concept. Baseball pitchers, for example, frequently talk about the need to "stay within themselves" when they want to block out any impact that the batter, the base stealer, or the crowd might have on their ability to perform at their best. This mental exercise coaches you on "staying within yourself" and "playing your zone" in your relationship. It shows you how to keep a positive mental focus on yourself—even in the face of your partner's grumpy moods or negative behavior. It will offer you a quick, easy method for maintaining your emotional independence.

Time: 10 minutes anytime—whenever you feel yourself losing your emotional independence or your positive focus on yourself.

Equipment Needed: A large mirror (bathroom mirror, hall mirror, etc.) and a kitchen timer or alarm clock.

Body Position: Sitting or standing.

* * *

Step 1: Find a mirror large enough for you to see your entire face in it, preferably in a room that's quiet, where you won't be disturbed. Sit or stand in front of this mirror. Set a timer or alarm clock for 10 minutes.

Step 2: Gaze at your reflection in the mirror for a few seconds. Then zero in on your eyes. Lock your focus into your eyes. Don't fuss over your makeup, examine your flaws, or fix your hair—keep your stare fixed on your eyes. By focusing intently on your eyes, you will be getting in touch with yourself, the personality that's reflected through the eyes. Now say aloud or to yourself: "I have the power to stay within myself." Repeat this sentence several times.

Step 3: After repeating the sentence several times and while keeping your gaze fixed on your eyes, take three deep breaths (inhale slowly through your nose, hold for 5 seconds, exhale slowly through your mouth). Continue to gaze into your eyes until the timer rings, but while doing so, begin to create your "personal zone" by formulating a statement of positive beliefs about yourself. This statement can be as lofty as an assertion of who you are and what you want to do with your life, or as mundane as a list of goals you want to accomplish that day. As you stare into your eyes, think positive thoughts about these goals, this "zone" you've created for yourself. If negative thoughts pop into your mind, such as, "But what will John think about my hopes of going back to school and getting my degree?" gently push them away by repeating the sentence "I have the power to stay within myself," and by refocusing your gaze on your eyes in the mirror.

Step 4: When the timer rings, say the sentence, "I have the power to stay within myself," once more. Blink your eyes several times, take a deep breath, stretch, and go on with your day.

Note: The next time you're in a situation where you feel yourself adapting your behavior to your partner's, or where your partner's negative attitude toward you drains your motivation, thereby pulling you out of your "personal zone," think back to the reflection of your eyes in the mirror and say the sentence, "I have the power to stay within myself."

4

Exercises for Adult-Child Relationships

Last year I needed a simple box of crayons and found myself in an enormous nationally franchised children's toy store. As I surveyed the aisles and aisles of product, it dawned on me that when a retailer devotes over 10,000 square feet to children's toys and assorted paraphernalia, it's serious business. Then I noticed that bookstores were devoting entire sections to children's titles as well as to books on baby names, infant care, child development, etc. Yes, I knew we were in the midst of a new baby boom, but until I started browsing in toy stores and bookstores, it hadn't occurred to me how very *serious* today's parents are about entertaining and educating their children.

The parents who come to my office, children in tow, are, for the most part, bright, educated, and eager to be the best parents they can be. They supplement their children's education with music lessons, they encourage them to try sports that emphasize personal development (like karate), they send the kids to summer camp to become computer literate as well as proficient in team sports, and they enroll them in programs that will help them perform well on college entrance exams—even when they are only freshmen in high school.

Today's parents are keenly interested in raising mentally,

as well as physically, fit children. That's why I've created a chapter of mental exercises for them. The issues addressed here are by no means *all* the child-rearing situations parents face, but they are representative of the type of topics parents often bring to my attention.

Learning how to listen to a child, disciplining a child without feeling guilty, heightening a child's mental powers, and averting power struggles with teenagers are among the subjects covered in this chapter. I hope parents, teachers, childcare professionals, and any adults who spend time with kids will use these exercises to achieve mental fitness for themselves and the children in their lives.

ADULT-CHILD RELATIONSHIP EXERCISE 1

Learning How to Listen to Children

Benefit: Children develop a positive, healthy mental outlook when the adults in their lives *really* listen to them. In other words, a child's ego development depends directly on the quality of the responses he or she gets over the years. A child who feels he or she is not being listened to will feel rejected, and the seeds of low self-esteem will be planted. This exercise is designed to help parents, teachers, counselors, older siblings, grandparents, or any adult "get into" the proper frame of mind to listen to a child.

Time: 5–10 minutes any time of day or night, preferably *before* any interaction with a child that's going to last more than 15 minutes (e.g., driving a child to school, helping a child with homework, getting a child ready for bed, etc.).

Equipment Needed: One sheet of black construction paper and one sheet of white construction paper.

Body Position: Any of your choosing.

*   *   *

Step 1: Write your name in the center of the sheet of black construction paper. Yes, it's barely readable, but that's part of the goal here. Pick up the paper and hold it approximately 6 inches in front of you. With your eyes open, think or say out loud everything that's going on with *you* that day (e.g., "I've got a dental appointment at three o'clock," "I've got to pick up my dry cleaning by six o'clock," "My boss has called an important meeting for this afternoon," etc.). Do this for as long as you need to in order to exhaust all the mental activity floating inside your head that concerns you. Think of this sheet of black paper as a movie screen onto which you're projecting all of your thoughts about yourself. The reason the screen is black is that you're switching off the lights on all mental activity that concerns you.

Step 2: Take the sheet of white construction paper and write the child's name ten to fifteen times in big letters all over the paper. Think or say out loud everything that's going on with *the child* (e.g., "Sarah was grumpy getting up this morning," "Sarah's science fair is coming up this weekend," "Sarah told me her friend was teasing her yesterday," etc.). Do this projecting as long as you need to until you find yourself totally immersed in Sarah's world. Think of *this* sheet of white paper as a movie screen onto which you're projecting all of your thoughts about the child. The reason this screen is white is that you're switching on the lights on all mental activity that concerns the child.

Step 3: If your mind begins to wander back to yourself as you're projecting onto the white paper, just pick up the black paper, project the thought onto the black screen, and put the black paper aside.

Step 4: You've completed the exercise when several minutes of uninterrupted "child thoughts" have been projected onto the white screen. Then simply put the child's sheet aside and use it again before your next interaction with him or her.

Step 5: If you're on your way to meeting the child at school, at the dentist, etc., and you become immersed in thoughts about yourself again, just think of the white paper and your focus will return to the child. You might even try making wallet-size versions of each paper (black and white) to carry with you everywhere.

Note: For those of you who are saying, "This is all well and good, but I'm a very busy person who is always getting distracted," I have this to say: No one expects you to stop functioning whenever a child appears. But do this exercise at least once a day. What will happen in a matter of days is that the quality and depth of your listening skills will increase dramatically and you will make a positive impact on any child with whom you interact.

ADULT-CHILD RELATIONSHIP EXERCISE 2

Disciplining a Child Without Guilt

Benefit: Many of the parents who come to me for counseling share the same problem: They have great difficulty disciplining their children without feeling guilty. Many of the children who are brought to me because they're "disciplinary nightmares" share the same problem: They have not been reared with consistent disciplinary boundaries. What's going on here? Two things. First, today's two-career couples are feeling tremendously conflicted over the lack of quality time they're able to spend with their children and, therefore, swing between gross leniency and discipline born out of frustration and fatigue. Second, the majority of the parents I counsel are between the ages of twenty-five and forty-five—

the generation of men and women who were raised in the baby boom era by parents who were too lenient themselves and unwittingly created egocentric "me-first" kids. These "kids" are today's parents, so it's not surprising that they're to lenient with *their* kids. To these parents, discipline is synonymous with "punishment" or "abuse." As a result, they suffer great pangs of guilt when they're forced to impose rules and consequences on their children. But the truth is, discipline is simply setting boundaries. The *purpose* of imposing discipline is to enable children to adapt their behavior to their immediate environment—whether it's home, school, church, or a shopping mall. The *importance* of imposing discipline is to give a child the emotional and behavioral framework to become an adult who is responsible in every way—to himself, to his family and friends, to his community, and to the world at large. This mental exercise will teach parents how to free themselves from the cycle of discipline-guilt-remorse-leniency-frustration-anger-discipline.

Time: 10–15 minutes for preparation and another 1–5 minutes for the exercise, which may be performed day or night, whenever needed.

Equipment Needed: Pen, a half dozen sheets of paper, and a glass jar or other see-through container (one for each child, if you have more than one).

Body Position: As the exercise dictates.

* * *

Step 1: Take one sheet of paper and list the basic concepts you wish to teach your child as he or she grows up (e.g., #1 bathing and grooming, #2 respect for authority; #3 household chores; #4 traffic safety, etc.). You can always add to this list later on and create different lists for different children.

Step 2: Take the additional sheets of paper and cut them into squares large enough to write short phrases on them (fifty to sixty squares approximately 2 inches by 2 inches in size).

Step 3: Write one of your concepts on each of the squares that you cut out (i.e., print "bathing and grooming" on one square, "respect for authority" on another, etc.). You will have lots of blank squares left over for future use.

Step 4: Place all the squares in a drawer, folder, or box that is easily accessible.

Step 5: Place the glass jar somewhere where you will pass by it several times a day. Label it with the child's name. (If you have more than one child, do the same with an individual jar for each child.)

Step 6: Before we continue, here's an example of how this exercise works. Let's say Jennifer, whose household chores include taking care of the pets, has forgotten to feed the cat for two days in a row. You've already explained to her that the next time she shirks her responsibilities, she'll have to go to bed early for as many nights as the cat was neglected. You call her to the kitchen, tell her what she's done, and impose the disciplinary rule. Jennifer whines, cries, and says how unfair, mean, and cruel you are as she stomps off to her room. This is the point where most parents experience feelings of guilt and engage in an internal dialogue that sounds like: "I only get to see her a few hours a day and now I've sent her to her room." Or: "She's only eight years old, so she can't be expected to do everything right." As these thoughts and feelings begin to surface, go immediately to your drawer or folder and pull out the square on which the concept you are currently trying to teach your child is printed. (If you find yourself disciplining your child for a concept you've forgotten to put on your list, write it on a blank square now.) In Jennifer's case, "household chores" is the concept. Take a few minutes to remind yourself why you believe this concept is important for your child's development.

Step 7: Now take the square, go to the jar with Jennifer's

name on it, and drop it inside. The point here is, rather than *taking something away* from your child by disciplining her, you're making a *contribution* to her development. Whenever you're feeling guilty about disciplining your child over the next few days and weeks, look over at the jar and observe how many "deposits" you've made into your child's emotional future—and *feel good about it!* An empty jar means either that your child is perfect or you aren't assuming *your* responsibilities as a parent.

Note: An added benefit of this exercise is that it often teaches parents something about themselves. For example, if you find yourself continually disciplining your child for concepts not found on your list, perhaps you're being arbitrary or you're simply too tired or short-tempered. This exercise is a good way to monitor your own behavior, especially because you must articulate exactly why you are disciplining your child by writing the concepts on your list and on the squares.

Teaching Parents to Make Time for Themselves

Benefit: How do working parents juggle raising children, holding down a job, and managing a household? Not very well, according to the stressed-out parents who come to me for counseling. Their situation can be summed up in one word: overload! They put in a grueling day at the office, only to come home to *more* responsibilities and pressures. It's enough to make any parent frazzled—and frazzled parents create frazzled children. What's the solution? I tell my clients that in order to be better parents, they *must* take quality time for themselves. I know it seems impossible to squeeze in "me-time" between work, school, piano lessons, little league games, and grocery shopping, but taking 10-20 minutes a day for pure, unmitigated *self-care* will go a long way toward replenishing a parent's emotional resources. Remember, you're not neglecting your children if you take time for yourself—you're nurturing that part of you that's a person first and a parent second. And if you don't believe me, just ask your kids which version of you they'd rather deal with— the parent who's physically and emotionally drained or the parent who's calm and collected? This exercise can be squeezed into any parent's schedule. It has only three steps and is simple to do. Most important, it forces you to make time for yourself by asking you to *filter out* all your conflicting chores, responsibilities, and parental pressures and *focus on* yourself for at least 10 minutes a day. As a parent, your mental energy is constantly flowing outward. This exercise gives you—the person—the opportunity to focus your mental energy inward.

Time: 5–10 minutes. Do this exercise whenever you're on overload.

Equipment Needed: Pen and paper.

Body Position: Sitting comfortably.

* * *

Step 1: Take a sheet of paper and on the top left-hand side, write your name. Next to your name, write one of your parental chores, commitments, or concerns (e.g., "Susan—preparing for daughter's private school interview"). Keep writing your name and whatever parental activities are sapping your mental energy, as illustrated by the following:

> Susan—preparing for daughter's private school
>   interview
> Susan—dropping off dry cleaning
> Susan—shopping for daughter's school clothes
> Susan—calling son's little league coach

Step 2: Keep writing as quickly as you can, without stopping to analyze or internalize the activities and pressures you're listing. Stop only when you feel you've exhausted your list of competing focuses. However, do not stop writing your *name* until you can write it ten times without flashing back to your parental pressures, as illustrated by the following:

> Susan—preparing for daughter's private school
>   interview
> Susan—dropping off dry cleaning
> Susan—shopping for daughter's school clothes
> Susan—calling son's little league coach
> Susan—handling sibling fights
> Susan—making dinner
> Susan
> Susan
> Susan
> Susan
> Susan
> Susan
> Susan

Susan
Susan
Susan

Step 3: When you can write your name ten times without focusing on your role as a parent, stop writing. Take a deep breath and count slowly from 1 to 100. After each group of five numbers, say your name (e.g., "1-2-3-4-5-Susan," "6-7-8-9-10-Susan," etc.). When you reach "100-Susan," stop and take another deep breath. You have just relieved yourself of the stress caused by all your parental burdens and have taken time to nurture yourself.

Note: This exercise can also be performed in your head, without using pen and paper. The point is to filter out all the chores, activities, and obligations that contribute to your parental overload and encourage you to make time for yourself.

ADULT-CHILD RELATIONSHIP EXERCISE 4

Heightening a Child's Mental Powers

Benefit: One of the dilemmas facing today's parents, teachers, and child-care professionals is this: In our age of mindless TV shows and addictive video games, how can we motivate our children to exercise their brains without experiencing burnout? Children *want* to use their brains. They're naturally curious about the world around them, and they want to be more competent in dealing with their environment. It's up to us adults to find ways to stimulate children, tap their potential, and unlock their unique skills and talents. This exercise is designed to help you inspire children ages eight and up to use their minds to the fullest. It's a "brain game" to be played by you and your child, and because it's a game, there are no right or wrong answers—just mental play. Before he or she knows it, your child will be amazed at how much fun learning can be!

Time: 10–15 minutes, day or night.

Equipment Needed: A dictionary of your choice—either a Webster's or one that's geared specifically for children.

Body Position: As the exercise dictates.

* * *

Step 1: Tell your child you want to play a game with him or her—a game that will use a word in several different ways. Explain that the game is for *fun only;* that there are no scores, no winners, and no losers.

Step 2: Take out the dictionary. Ask your child to close her eyes and flip through the pages. As she's doing this, you'll count from 1–5. When you reach 5, say "Stop." She should stop flipping the pages and pause on a single page. Tell her to keep her eyes closed. Then ask her to point anywhere on the page.

Step 3: Ask her to open her eyes and read the word she's found. (Assist her if the word is one that's long or difficult to pronounce.) Then ask her to read the definition of the word. If necessary, discuss the definition with her so she understands its meaning or meanings.

Step 4: Now ask the child to try spelling and pronouncing the word backward (i.e., if the dictionary word is "juggler," the answer will be "relgguj"). When spelled backward, most words sound funny, and your child will enjoy repeating the odd-sounding word.

Step 5: Now ask her to make up a definition for this "pretend" word (e.g., "Relgguj means puppy dog in Martian language").

Step 6: Now ask your child to go back to the original dictio-

nary word (e.g., "juggler") and try to think of words that begin with each letter in that word, as in the example below:

j—jelly bean   l—lizard
u—umbrella   e—ear
g—garage   r—radio.
g—gigantic

Step 7: To finish the game, ask your child to take the words she thought up in Step 6 and construct an entire sentence around them. The sentence doesn't have to make sense (the sillier the better), but it must be grammatically correct, as in the example below:

"I lifted up the *garage* door and saw a *gigantic jelly bean* standing under an *umbrella,* listening to the *radio,* and wearing headphones on his *lizard ears.*"

Note: An eight-year-old child will be sufficiently challenged by this exercise, no matter how many times he performs it. But an older child may need additional stimulation and motivation to perform it again and again. Here are a few ways to make the game more of a mental stretch for older kids:

- Ask them to make up *two* definitions for the dictionary word-spelled-backward instead of one, as in Step 5.
- Suggest that they complete the exercise by a specific time or deadline (set alarm or stop watch).
- If they've been studying a second language in school and are sufficiently proficient in it, have them list the words in Step 6 in that language.

Feel free to experiment with the Steps in this exercise as your child's abilities dictate.

ADULT-CHILD RELATIONSHIP EXERCISE 5

Bolstering a Child's Self-Esteem

Benefit: All children suffer pangs of self-doubt at one time or another, whether they're wondering if they'll make the basketball team, score high marks on their report card, or be accepted by the "in" group at school. The fact is, a child's life is fraught with tests—physical, intellectual, and emotional—

and his level of self-esteem is determined, in part, by how well he performs on these life tests. But we as parents, educators, and caretakers can help bolster a child's self-esteem by sharing the following exercise with him. Do this exercise whenever you sense that the child is measuring his worth in *external* measurements (school grades, number of party invitations, etc.). The purpose of the exercise is to pull the child's focus away from such external measurements and draw it toward *internal* attributes (sense of humor, responsible nature, etc.) in order to imbue the child with a real and lasting sense of self-esteem. Once you and the child have practiced the exercise together several times, you can encourage him to perform it himself, whenever he thinks his self-esteem needs bolstering.

Time: 10–20 minutes.

Equipment Needed: None

Body Position: As the exercise dictates.

* * *

Step 1: On the count of 10, ask the child to close his eyes. Now tell him that you and he are going to take five deep breaths (inhale through nose, hold for 5 seconds, exhale through mouth). The child's eyes should remain closed for the remainder of the exercise.

Step 2: Ask the child to picture a dark night sky. Then ask him to pretend to write his name in big white letters in this dark night sky.

Step 3: Tell him that you and he are going to put twinkling stars in the sky, all around his name, and that each star will represent a wonderful and very special "inner light" of his personality.

Step 4: You go first by describing two or three things about him that are positive, loving, or praiseworthy (e.g., "I can think of three things right away, Johnny: your kindness to animals, your friendly smile, and your skill at skateboarding"). Each time you mention an "inner light," ask him to imagine a new star next to his name in the sky.

Step 5: Now ask him to take a turn at adding stars to the sky by naming some positive qualities about himself. If he's hesitant out of shyness, boredom, or negativity, help him out by telling him that *any* good quality, big or small, will add stars to the sky; then name more of his "inner lights" (e.g., "You help with the dishes and you're considerate to your grandparents"). Try to get him to name some of his good qualities, and each time he does, tell him to place another star next to his name in the sky.

Step 6: Repeat Step 4, where you name more of his good qualities and tell him to add stars in the sky. Then repeat Step 5, where he names the qualities and adds more stars.

Step 7: Ask the child to name one last thing—the thing he *most* likes about himself—and tell him to make this star the biggest one in the sky.

Step 8: Tell him that any time he wants to feel good about himself, all he has to do is close his eyes and see his stars next to his name in the sky. Tell him he can add more stars each time he does the exercise. Then count from 1–10 and have him open his eyes.

Note: I know several children who are so "sold" on this simple mental game that whenever they're out at night and look up in the sky, they see the stars, remember all their good qualities, and feel good about themselves.

Averting Power Struggles With Teenagers

Benefit: As a therapist, I'm often called upon to mediate "wars of wills" between parents and teenagers. Such wars seem inevitable, but why? First, because kids—even the most stable, well-adjusted kids—experience a physical, mental, and emotional metamorphosis between the ages of twelve and fourteen. Their hormones go wild, and they turn into insensitive, disrespectful, junk-food-eating aliens practically overnight! I remind parents that there's absolutely nothing they can do about this metamorphosis, so they shouldn't try. However, they *can* do something about the second cause of parent-teen wars: They can realize that, after being total autocrats for the last twelve to fourteen years, they're resisting the idea of sharing their power with their budding adults, and, as a result, they're trying to exert *more* control over their teens instead of less. I know you're probably saying to yourself, "How can I share power with someone whose moods change on the hour?" My answer is that if a parent doesn't begin to share his power, his teen *will* struggle for it. The way to avert a power struggle with a teenager is to acknowledge his position on an issue while *calmly* maintaining yours. This mental exercise offers a six-step scenario that, when used during a confrontation with a teen, will guide you smoothly through those turbulent tangles over curfews, dating, driving, etc.

Time: 1 minute to review the six-step scenario below.

Equipment Needed: None.

Body Position: As the exercise dictates.

*   *   *

Step 1: Let's say the subject under discussion is weekend curfew times. Your first step should be to *give the floor to your* *teen*. Ask what he thinks about the issue. Ask for his reasons for his position. Don't interrupt. Listen. If he gives a one-line answer like, "I just want to," tell him you'd like to hear more of his thoughts on the subject.

Step 2: Your second step should be to *acknowledge the points he's made*. Tell him you understand his position (e.g., "You're saying the fun doesn't start until after midnight, so you don't want to be home by eleven-thirty").

Step 3: Your third step should be to *state your position calmly, simply, and directly*. Give him some reasons for your position, just as you asked him to give you reasons for his.

Step 4: Your fourth step should be to *point out areas where you're in agreement and ask him if he notices any* (e.g., Teen: "You're afraid I'll get into trouble if I stay out late." Parent: "You're right. I'm concerned about that").

Step 5: Your fifth step should be to *make a decision about the issue*. If you can negotiate a compromise, fine. If not, stick to your original position and explain why.

Step 6: There are two possibilities for this last step. If you've negotiated a compromise on the issue, your sixth step should be to *designate the teen as the one who will accept responsibility for the mutual decision* (e. g., "I'm putting you in charge of carrying out our decision"). Or, if you've decided to stick with your original position, your sixth step should be to *inform him that he should try to accept your decision with the best attitude possible* (e.g., "I know you're not happy with this decision, but I'm hoping you'll make it work for you").

Note: This exercise is not intended for adults who are dealing with a seriously troubled teenager. If you suspect that your son or daughter is suffering from drug or alcohol abuse, exhibiting suicidal behavior, or facing a major crisis of some kind, you should seek professional help for your teenager and yourself.

5

Exercises for
General Mental Fitness

Each exercise in this chapter addresses a common, universally shared problem, and each exercise will help readers approach life with a strong, healthy mind. By performing these exercises regularly, readers will achieve total mental fitness—a state that will enable them to feel capable, in charge, and ready for any challenge that lies ahead.

Topics covered in this chapter are: how to deal with the minor frustrations that crop up every day (is there anyone who wouldn't like to handle frustration better?); how to face grief, loss, or disappointment, whether it's the loss of a loved one or the loss of a job; how to focus positively on finances instead of worrying about them; how to stop that nasty mental habit known as procrastination; and how to learn patience, a real challenge for those of us who want what we want *now*!

GENERAL MENTAL FITNESS EXERCISE 1

Overcoming Minor Daily Frustrations

Benefit: Repeated performance of this exercise will allow you to glide over or through any number of minor daily frustrations, from traffic jams and canceled appointments to household appliances going on the blink and work projects going awry. You can't stop frustrating events from happening, but you *can* learn how to stop the negative effects of frustration from draining your mental and emotional energies. (Are you aware that the average person who lets feelings of frustration affect his mental outlook loses approximately 2–3 *hours a day* in mental energy that could otherwise be focused more positively?) I taught this exercise to a group of salespeople, who reported that within a week of using it even the most high-strung member of the group had experienced great improvement in his ability to deal with frustration. I've also taught the exercise to professional athletes, who use it in competition. The best way to describe the benefit of this exercise is that it will teach you how to get on with your day almost immediately after you experience the frustrating event.

Time: 5–10 minutes, depending on the level of frustration you're experiencing. Begin the exercise the minute you feel yourself losing your cool.

Equipment Needed: None.

Body Position: Whatever position you happen to be in when the frustration or setback occurs. You can perform this exercise while running, walking, talking, etc.

* * *

Step 1: As we walk through this exercise, let's use the example of a minor auto accident. Your car has just suffered a fender bender and your mind is spinning in several directions. "Great," you say to yourself. "Now I'll be late for the meeting . . . I don't know what my deductible is . . . That jerk wasn't even looking where he was going when he backed into me . . ." and so on. Your first step is to stop this parade of thoughts as soon as you feel yourself getting hot under the collar. But continue whatever physical activity you were doing (getting out of the car, reaching for your insurance card, whatever).

Step 2: This next step is called "witnessing," and it takes a bit of explaining the first time around. The difference between a "witness" and a "judge" is that a witness simply gives his description of what he observes happening at any given time, whereas a judge gives his *opinion* of what he's observing. European sports announcers covering a tennis match generally describe the action simply as it occurs ("Now the ball is being hit to the server's backhand service court, and now it is being returned as a drop shot"). American sports announcers, on the other hand, often give us their *opinions* or *judgments* of how the match is going, along with their observations ("Connors has just served a double fault; he must be tired after playing a grueling three-set match yesterday"). In Step 2, you decide to become a witness—not a judge—to your own actions during your fender bender incident.

Step 3: Begin to describe out loud or to yourself every physical movement you make for the next 5–10 minutes, as if you were an announcer covering the play-by-play of your fender bender incident. Simply describe what you're doing and leave out all judgments ("I'm opening up the glove compartment to look for my insurance card and I'm finding that it's not there. Now I'm opening up my wallet and looking for it there. Now I have the card in my hand and I'm opening the car door and walking over to the car that struck mine. Now I'm asking the man for his information.") Stop witnessing when you begin talking to the man, then continue the process with "Now I'm looking around for a phone booth to report the accident to the traffic police. I'm getting a quarter out of my pocket, putting it in the slot, and dialing the operator." You get the idea. The point is to simply be a witness to your own actions. You are describing the physical activity you see yourself performing (witnessing), *not* describing the emotions you are having (judging). Here's how the judge would describe the same incident: "I'm looking in the glove compartment for the damn card but it's not in there. Where the hell is it? I'm so mad I could kill someone. Now I'm walking over to the jerk who caused all this and he'd better have his insurance information available right away . . ."

Step 4: After approximately 5–10 minutes of witnessing your frustrating situation, check your level of frustration. You should notice that your *feelings* of frustration have lessened considerably or even disappeared. If not, you may want to continue doing the exercise, regardless of how many minutes have passed—Stop whenever *you* no longer feel frustrated.

Note: Clients are always amazed by how well this exercise works and they often want to know exactly *how* it works. Simple. As you begin to focus your mind on the physical aspects of the event and take your mind off your feelings related to the event, your feelings, which are no longer being given any attention, "die" of their own accord. Feelings stay alive and kicking only when you've given them mental energy or attention. Sometimes clients will say, "But I *want* to pay attention to my feelings." I explain that there are lots of times in life when we need to and should pay attention to our feelings, but living through a time of frustration is not one of them.

GENERAL MENTAL FITNESS EXERCISE 2

Facing Grief, Loss, or Disappointment

Benefit: We've all suffered losses—of jobs, material possessions, and, most painfully, loved ones. This exercise uses the power of the mind to recreate the intense feeling of grief under controlled conditions, so that we can accelerate the normal grieving process and move on after the loss. This is a powerful exercise that will trigger painful emotions, so reserve it for what I call "large and important losses," not for daily frustrations or minor disappointments. During the exercise you will confront the loss and eventually feel the grief ebbing away, until it no longer depresses you and keeps you from functioning normally. No mental exercise can eliminate the pain of loss, but this exercise will give you an overall sense of control over the pain, as you begin to realize that *you* can choose the time and place when you will feel the pain, not vice versa.

Time: As I mentioned, this is a powerful exercise. So choose a time after which you can relax and not feel pressured to rush back to your daily routine. If you perform the exercise during the evening, be sure it's completed at least 3 hours before bedtime. Allow 15–20 minutes or longer, if needed, for the exercise.

Equipment Needed: Kitchen timer or alarm clock.

Body Position: Sitting and lying down. Choose a dark and relatively quiet location. Turn off lights, shut doors, and pull the drapes.

*   *   *

Step 1: Take twenty deep breaths (inhale through your nostrils, hold for 5 seconds, exhale slowly through your mouth). Close your eyes, if you wish.

Step 2: Lie on your back and lift your legs as high as you can, supporting your legs and back with your arms. If you have back problems and can't perform this "shoulder stand," lie on your back on the floor near a bed or sofa and rest your legs on the mattress or cushion. The point here is to allow blood to move gently to the brain. Stay in this position from 1–5 minutes. Stop if you feel any sensation of pounding or throbbing. (If you can do an actual headstand, great.) Then sit up.

Step 3: Set the timer or alarm clock for 15–20 minutes and place it nearby so you can hear it ring. Tell yourself this time has been set aside for confronting grief and loss. Push away any distracting thoughts. Begin to construct a sentence that *names* your loss (if it's a person, say his name; if it's a job, name the position).

Step 4: In your mind list the reasons this person or event was important to you. Take as much time as you need to think of the various losses this situation represents. Be graphic and complete in your descriptions. Don't hesitate to state the loss in the most maudlin terms (e.g., "Jim was the only man who ever loved me").

Step 5: Conjure up any thoughts of anger, surprise, or shock that surround the subject of your loss (e.g., "How could he have left me this way?"). If you begin to cry, let yourself cry. Don't stop it. Let the feelings come—simply notice them as they arise.

Step 6: Picture or remember any times—positive or negative—that you shared with this person or experienced in this situation. But try not to organize your thoughts; if your mind floats back to a certain scene, let it.

Step 7: Allow any feelings of hopelessness, despair, or sadness to come forward. These feelings have no power over you; they are just feelings. Stay in this step as long as you can.

Step 8: Now say to yourself, "This is the sadness and grief that I feel whenever I think of my loss. I will allow these feelings and thoughts to come forward from time to time, but only when *I* choose to do this exercise. *I* control where and when they are to be confronted. As I complete this exercise, I choose to leave these feelings and thoughts behind in this grieving room. I will not take them with me when I leave the room."

Step 9: When the timer rings, open your eyes if they were shut. Get up and turn on lights and open doors. Take a look around the room and let your eyes rest on familiar objects. Take a few deep breaths. Count from 1 to 100. Begin to tune back into your day.

GENERAL MENTAL FITNESS EXERCISE 3

Training Your Mind to Focus Positively on Finances

Benefit: The subject of money—making it or not having it—is probably always on your mind, no matter what your financial means. Whether you think about stretching the family budget, saving up for your first home, or being able to afford an extravagant vacation, the issue of money uses up an enormous chunk of your mental energy. It's in your best interest, then, to focus *positively* on your finances, rather than worry about them, even in bleak economic times. Worrying doesn't solve financial problems—it only makes them worse. How can you focus positively on money, given the financial pressures many people face in the nineties? By training your mind to think in terms of *attracting financial abundance.* The more often you think about achieving a goal, the more energy you direct toward achieving that goal. Or, as the New Age gurus might put it, "If you think thoughts of financial abundance, you'll draw those vibrations into your life." This mental exercise is intended to do just that—to draw a positive attitude toward money into your life. It is *not* designed to help you get rich quick. It *is* designed to focus your mind on financial success, to give you the attitude of "I have" instead of "I wish." However, if you're too worried about your financial situation to even *begin* to think positively about money, refer to the Cooling Down chapter at the end of this book. The exercises there may help alleviate your anxiety. If it's your low self-esteem that's inhibiting your ability to focus positively on your finances, try performing the exercise in the Romantic Relationships chapter called "Repairing Self-Esteem After Rejection." If you've suffered a recent financial loss and have had trouble coping with that loss, refer to the exercise in the General Mental Fitness chapter called "Facing Grief, Loss, or Disappointment." It will help you face up to your loss and enable you to move ahead with the exercise in this chapter.

Time: 1–5 minutes preparation and another 1–2 minutes for the exercise, which may be done as many times as needed, day or night.

Equipment Needed: Pen and paper.

Body Position: As the exercise dictates.

* * *

Step 1: *Preparation.* Take a few minutes to think about a specific amount of money that you need or want in your life for a particular purpose (to pay bills, buy a car, etc.). Insert this amount into the following sentence and write the completed sentence on the sheet of paper: "I attract $_____ into my life with positive intent and thoughts of abundance."

Step 2: Place this sheet of paper (your "financial credo") where you can easily glance at it several times a day. (Some clients like to make copies of the credo and place them in three to five different locations around their home or office). At least three times a day, glance at the credo, read it, and repeat it to yourself several times.

Step 3: Throughout your day—while working, driving your car, shopping, etc.—allow your mind to focus on *numbers* that remind you of the numerical amount you chose for your credo. Let's say your sentence reads, "I attract $5,000 into my life with positive intent and thoughts of abundance." Any time you see or hear the number 5 in a phone number, on a street sign, in a sales report, or in your child's math homework, allow your mind to use this numerical trigger to focus positively on your amount of $5,000. Then repeat the credo to yourself several times.

GENERAL MENTAL FITNESS EXERCISE 4

Combating Procrastination

Benefit: How many times have you vowed to start a diet, clean a closet, or write a report, only to put off the task for days or even weeks? Many, undoubtedly. Everyone suffers bouts of procrastination, that pesky yet powerful desire to delay, defer, or avoid tackling a project or activity. Procrastination has nothing to do with laziness; even high achievers procrastinate. And it has nothing to do with the grimness of the task; people procrastinate even on projects they *know* will yield positive results. So when does procrastination rear its ugly head? Whenever you focus on your *thoughts* about an activity rather than on the actual *doing* of it. Thoughts—and the feelings they trigger—can overwhelm you to the point of emotional paralysis. They conjure up images that scare you into putting off the very project you want and need to do. The only way to combat these thoughts is to develop your ability to *do* and not to *think*. This exercise helps you do that by imposing specific deadlines on routine tasks. You will learn how to focus on the tasks themselves, rather than on your thoughts and feelings about them.

Time: 1–15 minutes anytime, day or night.

Equipment Needed: Alarm clock or kitchen timer.

Body Position: As the exercise dictates.

* * *

Step 1: Think about your daily routine, select five to ten simple tasks or chores you'd normally perform, and assign each one a time limit by which you can reasonably complete the task (e.g., "iron shirt—5 minutes"; "unload dishwasher—3 minutes"; "groom pet—10 minutes"; etc.). You can either keep this list in your mind or write it down.

Step 2: Before you begin each task, set the timer for the time you've assigned. Start each task by saying out loud or to yourself, "On the count of 5, I will start. 1-2-3-4-5-begin."

Step 3: Don't worry if negative thoughts and feelings creep into your mind as you perform each task; just focus on the timer and on completing the task before it rings. If you find yourself finishing your tasks well before the alarm rings, chop a minute or two off the allotted time the next time you set the timer. (Most procrastinators have unrealistic ideas about how long tasks take—most tasks will take less time than you think!) If the alarm rings before you've finished your task, simply reset it and keep going. The important thing is to *complete the task!*

Step 4: After you've performed five to ten timed tasks (whether over the course of one day or one week), begin to apply the technique of this exercise to the project you've been avoiding. In other words, think about the project and assign it a definite time limit or deadline. Examples include: "By the end of the day on Monday, I will have filled out and mailed all my change of address cards." Or: "On Tuesday I'll draft my resume and on Wednesday I'll type it up." Or: "In 45 minutes I will have organized my closet." As you begin to tackle each task, say to yourself or out loud, "On the count of 5, I will start. 1-2-3-4-5-begin." If your mind drifts to thoughts and feelings of how unpleasant, difficult, or dull the project is, focus on your deadline and on completing the project within the allotted time.

GENERAL MENTAL FITNESS EXERCISE 5

Learning Patience

Benefit: A common malady among my overachieving, goal-oriented clients is a problem that's all too prevalent among people living and working in the nineties: a gross lack of patience. Actually, it's not surprising that people lack patience in a world of automatic coffee makers, microwave ovens, and television sit-coms in which complex issues are resolved in a half hour. What this "instant gratification society" has produced is a group of hardworking, motivated people who have little control over their own impulses as well as unrealistic standards for themselves and others. This mental exercise is for people who *recognize* their lack of patience and wish to do something about it. It will not lessen your drive or motivation; what it will do is strengthen your mastery over yourself. All the "champions" I've worked with—professional athletes and corporate managers alike—have learned patience, which I define as the ability to stop and wait for personal desires to be fulfilled. A top tennis player uses patience to wait for the right moment to make a shot. A CEO uses patience to wait until the marketplace is ready for a new idea. *You* can use patience in a variety of ways—whether controlling your desire to eat or waiting to be hired for a new job. Remember that having patience doesn't mean sitting and watching the world go by; it means possessing a kind of self-control that, when used wisely, can improve the quality of your life. By performing this mental exercise, you will learn how to *interrupt* an activity (this will teach you how to "let go" of your desires and impulses) and learn how to *wait* for an event to occur (this will teach you how to delay gratification). Both concepts—interrupting and waiting—are the key components of patience.

Time: Throughout the day, 1–30 minutes depending on the activity. Try performing two to three *interrupting* activities and two to three *waiting* activities per day for two to three weeks. If that's too easy for you, try doubling the number of activities.

Equipment Needed: As the activity dictates.

Body Position: As the activity dictates.

* * *

Instead of following sequential steps, simply read over the

sample situations below (or create situations of your own) and perform two or three a day from each category.

Sample Situations for Learning How to *Interrupt* an Activity:

1. While listening to a song you like on the radio or stereo, switch stations or turn off the stereo in the middle of the song. Don't go back to the station until you're sure the song is over. (The same principle applies to TV watching. I have a client who's a sport fan; he turns off the TV during the final minutes of a close basketball game! Now that's practicing self-control!)

2. In the middle of any household or office task (making beds, watering plants, organizing files, writing memos), stop and wait 30 minutes before returning to the task.

3. While reading a newspaper, magazine, or book, stop in the middle of a page and don't return to the story for 24 hours. (Obviously, don't chose reading material that's crucial to your job!)

4. While relaxing in a bath, on the sofa, or in a lounge chair, get up and return to work before you'd like to.

5. Carry a kitchen timer (or a watch with an alarm) with you for half a day. As you perform your daily activities, set it to go off every 30 minutes. When it rings, stop whatever you're doing, wait 3–5 minutes, and return to the activity. Then reset the alarm and repeat the exercise.

Sample Situations for Learning How to *Wait* For an Event:

1. While you're waiting in line at a restaurant or grocery store, purposely allow several people to be seated or checked out before you.

2. While driving your car, let several cars cut in front of you.

3. Whenever you're ready to eat a meal, stop and wait 30 minutes before beginning.

4. Choose an appointment you've scheduled (dentist, lunch date, tennis game, etc.) and purposely arrive 30 minutes before you'd normally arrive. (If you like to arrive 30 minutes before your appointments, get there an hour early.)

5. Before getting on an elevator, let the elevator complete an entire cycle (i.e., let it go all the way up to the top floor and come down). If you're already being forced to wait for the elevator, wait an extra cycle.

Note: The *beauty* of this exercise is that as you're self-imposing interruptions and delays on your daily life, you're teaching yourself patience. The *lesson* of this exercise is that the world doesn't come to an end when you're forced to be patient. You'll find that your mind will learn to distract itself while you're waiting, and your desires and impulses will lose some of their dictatorial power over you. Then, you'll move easily from having patience in self-imposed situations to having patience when others interrupt or thwart you.

GENERAL MENTAL FITNESS EXERCISE 6

Controlling Fear

Benefit: Fear can be one of our most debilitating emotions, whether we're afraid of breaking a leg on the ski slopes or losing our job to a competitive coworker. Fear is an inevitable part of life, and while we can't avoid it entirely, we *can* reduce the level of fear we experience as well as the impact fear has on our minds and bodies. This exercise, which employs a technique known among psychologists as "paradoxical intent," forces you to face your fear and, thereby, control it. You will be asked to imagine that your worst fear comes true, over and over again, until your nervous system has become so desensitized to the fear that it's no longer disabled by it. You will experience mild to moderate discomfort while performing this exercise, as you will be activating your most dreaded and intense fear, but its long-term benefit is well worth the unpleasantness: You'll be able to control your fear and its significance in your life. Keep in mind that this exercise is *not* designed to cure paralyzing phobias and panic attacks or the physical symptoms that accompany them; those types of fear are best treated in a clinical setting by a trained professional. This exercise is also *not* intended to desensitize you to fears based firmly in reality (e.g., fear of walking in a crime-ridden neighborhood after dark); in those instances your mind is acting as a responsible guardian. This exercise *is* geared for people who want to manage the fears that cause them acute discomfort.

Time: 7 minutes once or twice a day. Give yourself four to six weeks to notice your diminished fear response. *SPECIAL NOTE:* don't do this exercise within 3 hours of bedtime; work on only one fear for four to six weeks; and don't do the exercise within 3 hours of a fear-provoking event (your nervous system needs to be "taught" the difference between the fear that's provoked externally and the fear that *you* provoke when you do this exercise).

Equipment Needed: Kitchen timer or alarm clock.

Body Position: Sitting or lying down.

* * *

Step 1: Choose a room where you can sit or lie down comfortably without being interrupted. Set a timer for 7 minutes and place it nearby so you can hear it ring.

Step 2: Close your eyes, count backward from 10–1, and ask yourself, "What is my worst fear?" Answer the question in a brief but descriptive manner (e.g., "I'm afraid of losing control when I swim in water where I can't see the bottom" or "I'm afraid my boyfriend will leave me for someone else").

Step 3: Now say to yourself, "I'm going to let myself imagine that my worst fear has come true, because *I* will decide when and where this fear upsets me, and I choose *this* time in *this* room." Until the timer rings, let your imagination conjure up the *worst* possible scenarios in which your fear comes true. Make these visualizations as vivid as possible. Allow yourself to really *feel* your fear, even if it makes you tremble or cry. The exercise only works if you feel discomfort. If what I call "protective happy thoughts" creep into your mind (e.g., "this isn't real, it's only pretend"), gently but firmly pull your attention back to your fear thoughts.

Step 4: When the timer rings at the end of 7 minutes, open your eyes and say to yourself, "The exercise is over. I will not allow these fear thoughts to return until I do this exercise again, because they are completely within my control."

Step 5: Take a few deep breaths. Then count from 1–100. Stand up, stretch, and go about your day.

GENERAL MENTAL FITNESS EXERCISE 7

Celebrating the Aging Process

Benefit: Age may be "just a state of mind," as the saying goes, but there are so many physical reminders of our advancing years (telltale gray hairs, wrinkles around the eyes, changes in body shape) that it's hard to keep the subject of age *off* our minds! And if the physical reminders aren't bad enough, there are the sociological and psychological reminders—like getting an invitation to your twentieth high school reunion, watching your son graduate from high school, or being asked by your son's high school friends if you've ever heard of Guns N' Roses! And then there's the issue of death, or, more specifically, the realization that life is not eternal. It's no wonder that we have such a negative attitude toward the aging process. But you *can* develop a positive mental outlook toward aging *without* buying a new sports car, surrendering to plastic surgery, or having an affair with a twenty-year-old. After performing this exercise regularly, you may even find yourself celebrating your advancing years! All you have to do is transform your "age crisis points" to "age power points." This exercise shows you how.

Time: 5–10 minutes anytime, day or night.

Equipment Needed: None.

Body Position: As the exercise dictates.

*   *   *

Step 1: Whenever you feel yourself at an "age crisis point," whether it's triggered by the sight of another gray hair, the fatigue of a hectic day, or the memory of your "lost youth," say "stop," take a deep breath, and count from 1–10.

Step 2: Take your chronological age and add the numbers together (for example, if you're forty-three years old, add 4 + 3 and come up with 7).This new number will be your "age power number."

Step 3: Now, let's say 7 is your age power number. For the next 3–10 minutes or so, think of 7 skills, accomplishments, experiences, or realizations you have had over the past 7 years that you are especially proud of—positive reminders of the power the years have brought you. This will be your "age power list." Examples are : 1) started doing aerobics; 2) overcame shyness on sales calls: 3) learned how to speak French; 4) volunteered to coach son's soccer team; 5) improved diet; 6) became district supervisor at work; 7) renovated kitchen.

Step 4: Take a minute or so to remember the circumstances and situations surrounding each item on your age power list.

Step 5: When you've finished compiling your mental list and have lingered briefly over each memory, snap back to the present by counting from 1–10 and repeating the credo, "My age brings me power and knowledge."

6

Cooling Down

The exercises in this final chapter of *Mental Aerobics* are designed to relax your mind and body. They show you how to let go of stresses and strains and sweep away the mental clutter that accumulates inside your mind during the day.

If you're like most of my clients, who understand the need for a balanced life but wonder how on earth to achieve one, these exercises offer specific methods.

What is a balanced life? It's a life filled with equal amounts of activity and rest. The "activity" part isn't the problem for most people; it's the "rest" part that's tricky—especially for people who are driven and goal-oriented. In fact, I tell my "Type A" clients that they may have to *work* at relaxation and be patient with themselves if it takes them time to become adept at it.

What is relaxation? It's being able to tune out the thousands of thoughts and feelings that race through our minds every day and reflect on nothing but calmness and serenity.

These cool-down exercises won't help you control the reams of paper that seem to flood your "in" box at work, nor will they make the myriad errands that demand your attention disappear. But they will teach you how to tune out and put aside your daily pressures—if only for 10 or 15 minutes at a time.

None of the exercises will make you feel so relaxed that you can't or won't want to complete the "must-do's" on your list. But they will give you a second—or third—wind, both mental and physical. Do them at the end of the day or whenever you feel the need to balance your life.

COOL-DOWN EXERCISE 1

Taking a Mental Catnap

Benefit: Have you ever wished you could close your eyes, shut out the world for a few minutes, and then return to it feeling rested and refreshed? I know a few lucky souls who can accomplish this by lying down, falling quickly into a deep sleep, and waking up 10–20 minutes later without an alarm clock. If you're on the go and can't afford to lie down and take a real nap in the middle of the day, this exercise is for you. It will allow you to have a "sanity break" in your physical and mental routine, whenever you feel the need to escape but don't have the time for a full-blown nap. It only takes 5 minutes to perform, and it can be done anywhere—at your desk, riding in a cab, or waiting in the doctor's office. And it won't put you into such a deep sleep that you'll be late for your next appointment! The state it *will* put you in is what I call restful dozing.

Time: 5 minutes anytime, day or night.

Equipment Needed: None.

Body Position: Sitting, standing, or lying down.

* * *

Step 1: With your eyes open, begin counting to 10, closing your eyes very *slowly* as you count. Take the full 10 seconds to close them, as if you were slowly drawing drapes. Don't worry if your eyelids start to flutter a bit; just keep pressing them down gently.

Step 2: When your eyelids are shut, say to yourself, "I am resting and dozing." Count to 10 in this closed-eye position.

Step 3: At the end of the 10 seconds, open your eyes, taking another 10 seconds to get them open completely. Count the seconds as you do this, imagining that you are opening drapes very slowly. When your eyes are fully open, say to yourself, "I am resting and dozing."

Step 4: Repeat Steps 1, 2, and 3. Perform this cycle of open-shut-open-shut ten times for a total of 5 minutes. Remember to repeat the phrase "I am resting and dozing" as you open and close your eyes. When you've completed the last cycle, blink your eyes quickly ten to twenty times. Then say, "I am fully awake now."

Note: As you perform this exercise, concentrate on your eyelids as they open and close. This will focus your attention on the act of resting, instead of on the pressures and stresses of your busy day.

COOL-DOWN EXERCISE 2

Staying in the Moment: A Mini-Meditation

Benefit: Meditation techniques drawn from such Eastern disciplines as Buddhism, Yoga, and Transcendental Meditation have been popular in the United States for years now, no doubt, because we've caught on to the fact that "stilling" our minds by staying in the moment can improve our mental and physical health—from relieving our anxiety to lowering our heart rate. Yet for all its obvious benefits, there are still millions of Americans who haven't given meditation a try. If you're among the uninitiated, here's your chance to experi-

prehensive:

ence the benefits of meditation firsthand. This cool-down exercise is a "mini-meditation," and it's simple to do. It will teach you how to still your mind so that your mental and physical energies will be focused on the calm of the present moment, rather than on the problems of the past or on the anticipated stresses of the future.

Time: 10–15 minutes, day or night.

Equipment Needed: A kitchen timer or alarm clock.

Body Position: Lying down.

* * *

Step 1: Lie down in a comfortable spot (bed, sofa, lounge chair). Set the timer for 10–15 minutes, depending on how much time you have. Place the timer nearby, so you can hear it ring.

Step 2: Count slowly from 1–10. At the count of 10, close your eyes gently.

Step 3: Take ten deep breaths (inhale slowly through your nose, hold for 5 seconds, exhale slowly through your mouth). Each time you inhale, think the word "still." Each time you exhale, think the word "now."

Step 4: After taking your deep breaths, breathe normally. Focus your attention on the sounds in the room. Listen closely and begin to name every sound you hear (car honking, police siren, clock ticking, bird singing, etc.). Don't think about how irritating the noises may be; just name the sounds to yourself. If you don't hear any sounds at all, go on to the next step.

Step 5: Rest your index and middle fingers gently on your upper lip, so that you can feel the subtle exhalation of air as you breathe out through your nose. Leave your fingers in this position for several minutes. Each time you inhale, think the word "still." Each time you exhale, think the word "now." Continue to breathe normally and feel the air on your fingers as you exhale. Don't try to create a big sensation on

your fingers; the sensation should be subtle.

Step 6: Now place one or both of your hands comfortably across your stomach, so that you can feel the rhythm of rising and falling as you breathe in and out. Stay in this position for several minutes. Each time you inhale and your stomach rises, think the word "still." Each time you exhale and your stomach falls, think the word "now." Breathe normally, even if your stomach rises and falls only slightly.

Step 7: Find a spot on your body where you can feel your pulse (your wrist, neck, etc.). With the same two fingers you used in Step 5, press the area firmly enough so you can feel the sensation of your pulse. Now count the pulses from 1–100. Don't attempt to adjust your breathing pattern to the rate of your pulse (your pulse will be faster); simply count 100 of your pulses.

Step 8: After 100 pulse beats, lay your hands comfortably at your sides. Until the timer rings, allow your mind to rest in the stillness you've created. If thoughts of business meetings, household chores, or other daily stresses creep in, gently erase them by thinking, "Still. Now."

Step 9: When the timer rings, count from 1–10, get up, stretch, and go on with your day.

COOL-DOWN EXERCISE 3

Relaxing With Color

Benefit: For those of you who aren't familiar with "color relaxation therapy," here's an exercise to introduce you to the concept. It draws on the fact that colors have major influences on our senses—positive and negative. Some people respond positively to "warm" colors such as red and orange; others react favorably to "cool" colors like blue and green. Even if you're not aware of your sensory predisposition to a particular category of colors, you're surely aware that some colors appeal to you and others don't. (If you wear blue clothes, drive a blue car, and sleep in a blue bedroom, it would be safe to say that blue evokes positive sensations for you. Conversely, if you rarely include red in your environment, then red is not a color to which you respond positively.) Since this exercise is designed to evoke positive—or, more specifically, relaxing—feelings in you, it uses only those colors you feel positive about. You'll be surprised at how your "positive" or favorite colors can help to soothe your frazzled nerves!

Time: Preparation time for this exercise is 1–2 minutes. How long you actually perform the exercise is up to you. (I suggest approximately 10 minutes, but by all means take as much time as you need to feel relaxed.) The exercise may be done anytime, day or night.

Equipment Needed: A kitchen timer or alarm clock, a sheet of white unlined paper, and a box of crayons.

Body Position: Lying down.

* * *

Step 1: *Preparation.* Take out your box of crayons and select a color you really like. (You may respond to different colors on different days, or you may choose the same color each time you do this exercise.)

Step 2: Color the entire sheet of white paper with the crayon you selected. Don't stop until you've achieved the exact shade you want (if you like deep red, press hard on your red crayon and go over the sheet of paper more than once). If you choose the same color each time you do the exercise, save this sheet of paper so you don't have to repeat this step each time.

Step 3: Now set the timer for 10 minutes or however long you think you'll need to relax. Lie down comfortably on a sofa, bed, or lounge chair. Prop up your color sheet in front of you, either by placing a pillow on your stomach and resting the sheet on it, by drawing your knees up toward your chest and resting the sheet on them, or simply by holding the sheet in your hands.

Step 4: Take five deep breaths (inhale through your nose, hold for 5 seconds, and exhale through your mouth).

Step 5: Focus your eyes on the center of your color sheet. Let your mind reflect on this color, let yourself focus on each memory association this color brings to mind. If your color is red, perhaps your memory associations will call up images of candy apples, red wagons, a Valentine heart, or red lipstick. Linger over each memory association, recalling specific incidents in which the color played a role (e.g., "Candy apples remind me of the carnivals my father used to take me to when I was a kid"). Spend time with each image until it fades away on its own. Let the images come and go naturally. During the exercise you may stay on one memory association or focus on ten different ones. It's up to you. You *should* pull your focus away from a memory if it begins to conjure up negative or upsetting emotions. However, the chances of this happening are slim, as you chose the particular color because of its positive associations for you.

Step 6: There may be times when no memory associations come to mind as you look at your color sheet. If that's the case, simply "rest" your eyes on the sheet and "sink" into the color as if it were a large pool.

Step 7: If your mind wanders off the sheet at any time during the exercise, refocus it by repeating the color's name ("red, red, red") until the memory associations return.

Step 8: When the timer rings, lay the sheet down. On the count of 20, get up, stretch, and return to your day.

COOL-DOWN EXERCISE 4

Dreaming While Awake

Benefit: Remember when you were a child and your parents read you bedtime stories? Remember how those tales of sugar plum fairies, singing bunny rabbits, and flying baby elephants sent you off to sleep feeling calm and secure? Child psychologists agree that positive, uplifting fantasy stories, read to children before bedtime, have a calming, restorative effect on children's minds, just as uplifting movies, books, and television programs help adults feel good about themselves and the world around them. Here's a simple cooldown exercise that encourages you to create your own fantasy stories or fairy tales. Try performing it at the end of a tough day; when you want to erase the strains of the past several hours, focus on thoughts of "sugar plum fairies," and drift off to a carefree, restful sleep.

Time: 10 minutes minimum.

Equipment Needed: None.

Body Position: Sitting or lying down.

* * *

Step 1: Sit or lie down in a place where you're not likely to be disturbed. Take off jewelry, loosen your tie, get comfortable. If you wish, turn on the radio to an easy listening station or play a tape of soothing background music.

Step 2: At the count of 10, close your eyes and take five deep breaths (inhale through your nose, hold for 5 seconds, exhale through your mouth). Keep your eyes closed for the remainder of the exercise.

Step 3: Now clear out images, thoughts, and feelings that have accumulated over the course of your day. You'll do this by imagining that you are watching a giant movie screen. Onto this screen you will project random scenes from your day (paying the electric bill, eating lunch with a friend, conducting a meeting in your office, etc.). Play out the scenes *quickly*, fast-forwarding as you go, until you reach the last random scene you can remember. Now flash the words "The End" on your screen. This final movie title represents the end of your day.

Step 4: Now you will decide what kind of fantasy story or fairy tale you wish to create for your mental viewing. Make your fantasy story a romantic saga, a swashbuckling adventure, a rousing comedy, or a spiritual drama. The nature and theme of this "movie" are entirely up to you and they may change daily. Once you've selected your movie of the day, go on to the next step.

Step 5: Begin showing your movie on the giant movie screen in your mind. Sit back and let the story unfold—whether the movie is a romance where the man of your dreams whisks you away from your humdrum routine and carries you off to his faraway castle, an action flick where you train for and win the Boston Marathon as your friends and family cheer you on, or a contemporary drama where you develop and market an exciting new product and become the toast of the Fortune 500 set! The only rule about this movie is that it must have an uplifting, inspirational theme that will evoke positive, happy feelings in you. In other words, good must triumph over evil, the good guys must finish first, etc. Play this movie a minimum of 10 minutes.

Step 6: When your movie is over, open your eyes. If you're in bed, take a few deep breaths, close your eyes, and drift off to sleep. If you are using this exercise as a simple method of relaxation and intend to continue with your daily routine, count to 10, get up, stretch, and go on with your day.

COOL-DOWN EXERCISE 5

Returning to Your Center

Benefit: This exercise takes all the "hot" emotions (anxiety, frustration, anger, etc.) that have accumulated during the day and dissipates their destructive energies before they can settle into your body. In addition to "cooling down" the mind, this exercise returns you to your "center" of being, the place from which all mental strength comes. This exercise is similar to those used by those who practice yoga.

Time: 10–15 minutes any time of day or night. A particularly good time to perform this exercise is after any kind of mental strain (studying for a test, meeting a deadline, etc.).

Equipment Needed: Kitchen timer or alarm clock.

Body Position: Lying down on a flat surface (a bed or floor) without a pillow to support your head.

* * *

Step 1: Set the timer or alarm clock for 10–15 minutes and place it nearby, so you can hear it ring.

Step 2: Close your eyes. Inhale deeply through your nose, hold for 5 seconds, and exhale slowly through your mouth until all the air is out. Repeat this deep breathing ten times, remembering to exhale through your mouth. After ten times, breathe normally and go on to the next step.

Step 3: With your index and middle fingers, find the exact center of your forehead and press down with both fingers.

Step 4: Keep your eyes shut tightly, with your eyeballs rolled back. Concentrate on keeping your eyelids closed throughout the exercise.

Step 5: Notice any and all colors that appear within the blackness. Think of the back of your eyelids as a large movie screen. Several of the following colors (yellow, orange, red, green, blue, purple, indigo, white) will appear in many shapes (circles, lines, swirls) within a few minutes.

Step 6: Simply watch the colors as you might watch a Technicolor movie or a laser light show. Your eyes may try to follow a pattern of colors as they float by, but try to keep your eyeballs rolled back and focused on the "screen." Don't think about anything—just watch the colors.

Step 7: If you begin to feel a sensation of "falling" into the blackness, go with the sensation. If, during the exercise, you start thinking of anything other than the colors, shut your eyes a little tighter; the colors will bring your attention back to the screen.

Step 8: When the timer rings, open your eyes gently. You will feel calmer, cooler, more collected, and more at peace. If you do this exercise at bedtime, you'll find yourself drifting off to sleep more smoothly and quickly.